The Anti-Defamation League's

Hate Hurts

How Children Learn and Unlearn Prejudice

Dear Readers,

Mention Laramie, Wyoming, Jasper, Texas, or Littleton, Colorado, and our collective conscience is assaulted by the brutal hate crimes committed in these places. We store in our mind's eye the image of five-year-old children clutching one another's hands as they run from a Jewish community day care center under attack by an anti-Semite. We are horrified by these images, sickened by them. Hate hurts, and we are all victims of the hate in our society. The seeds of hate that took root in Laramie and Jasper and Littleton exist everywhere ... in our communities, in our schools, even in our homes. Who among us has escaped being singled out, called names, or snubbed as a child or as an adult? Who has not heard an ethnic "joke" or a derogatory comment regarding someone's race or religion or sexual orientation?

Tragically, our children are often the first to reap the consequences of what we as a society have sown. They learn to hate before they are old enough to comprehend why. As parents and caregivers, we must teach our children not only to accept but to celebrate diversity. Intolerance is learned. Therefore it can be unlearned.

To further that objective, the Anti-Defamation League and Barnes & Noble have joined forces to launch a campaign called "Close the Book on Hate." We believe that through reading and discussion, children and their parents can better understand the richness and beauty of our multicultural society. This book, *Hate Hurts*, is an important first step. We encourage you to read it with your children and talk about its messages. Together we can make a difference.

Abraham H. Foxman　　　　**Leonard Riggio**
National Director　　　　　**Chairman**
Anti-Defamation League　　**Barnes & Noble, Inc.**

The Anti-Defamation League's

Hate Hurts

How Children Learn and Unlearn Prejudice

By Caryl Stern-LaRosa and Ellen Hofheimer Bettmann

SCHOLASTIC INC.

NEW YORK   TORONTO   LONDON   AUCKLAND   SYDNEY

MEXICO CITY   NEW DELHI   HONG KONG

Dedication & Thanks

This book is dedicated to our parents, Edwin and Manuela Stern, and Henry and Gertrude Hofheimer, for teaching us to value all people; and to our husbands, Donald LaRosa and Michael A. Bettmann, for their love and support. It is also dedicated to our children and grandchildren — Brian Hanway, Lee Terry, and James Edwin LaRosa; William Henry, Joanna Ellen, and Robert Ernst Bettmann; and Mackenzie and Zoe Bettmann-Adcock — for making the meaning of our work concrete and real.

Our heartfelt thanks to Abraham H. Foxman, National Director of the Anti-Defamation League, and Leonard Riggio, Chairman of Barnes & Noble, Inc., for providing us with the opportunity to create and promote this book. Thank you to Myrna Shinbaum and Mary Ellen Keating for their roles in bringing it all to fruition and to our ADL colleagues — both professional and lay leadership — for all that they have contributed to this book and to our lives in general. Special appreciation to Adrienne Ingrum and Sara Gearhart for their work and to our colleagues at Scholastic, especially our editor, Jean Feiwel, and also to Beth Levine, for making it all come together. Finally, to the thousands of children and adults who have participated in our A WORLD OF DIFFERENCE® Institute anti-bias workshops, thank you; your courage in the face of hate has touched our lives.

Contents

Contents

Part Two: Questions About Hate/ Responses to Hate

Contents

Part Three: Challenging Hate Outside the Home

Contents

Kids Do Experience Hate

"I am a brown-skinned girl, a mixture of Spanish, Japanese, and Filipino, who was born in San Francisco. When I started kindergarten, my family lived right in the city and my classmates were of all different colors and cultures. We all got along.

"In first grade, I moved to the suburbs, and suddenly everyone but me was white. The kids in my class teased me and kept asking me what I was. Finally, I asked my mom, 'What am I?'

"My mom said, 'You are a cosmopolitan — a person of the world.'

"I went back to school and told my classmates, 'I am a cosmopolitan. That means I am a person of the world.'

"My classmates were impressed that I knew such a big word. They stopped teasing me and started treating me with respect. Maybe they wanted to be cosmopolitans, too."

I f only it were always that simple. If only we could easily eliminate the pain our children experience when what makes them different also makes them the victim of teasing or even more serious acts of hate. Although the above story is true, it does not reflect the experiences most of us have had when we've tried to help our children understand that being different does not make them better or worse than others — just different. Most parents have faced this task without preparation. Although we want to help our children feel good about who and what they are and to value diversity, we often have little in the way of explanations or recommendations that will ease their pain.

Every day, in our cities and suburbs, small towns and countryside, in our classrooms and playgrounds and on our streets, our children are experiencing incidents and feelings such as those given below — the words and acts of prejudice and their effects, from the most subtle to the most violent:

"When I first came to this country, I had a problem speaking English correctly. I had an accent and they made fun of it."

"They were talking about ice-skating. I was hoping they would ask me to go with them. But they said, 'She can't ice-skate, she's Chinese.' (Well, I'm actually Korean, but they thought I was Chinese.) I bet I was probably better at skating than them — I was in group skating for two years. But they said, 'Chinese don't like sports. They don't want to go out. All they want to do is school. They want to look good in front of teachers.'"

"These two girls came along and they, like, pushed me out of the way. They just have these moods where one day they, like, really feel like beating somebody up, so they find a

white girl who's walking around, and they do."

Kids who have been the victims of prejudice not only suffer deeply themselves, they may also start causing others to suffer in return. Some report on how their own feelings and behavior toward "different" people changed after they'd been hurt:

"I got punched in the face, but that didn't really hurt me. The wounds heal. But they kept on calling me spic through the whole thing. I walk in the street and I feel lower.

"All this prejudice is starting to affect the way I feel about other people. I'm starting to be prejudiced myself."

"He actually spit in my sandwich . . . and said something like, 'I bet you're really hungry now, right? I bet you're really hungry now, black nigger — right? Right?'

"I've been through so much where prejudice is concerned, right now it's at the boiling point. It's, like, don't even think it . . . don't start it. You go your way and I'll go mine. Just leave me alone."

"He told me, 'My mother said I can't trust black people. I'm supposed to hate black people.'

"After a while I hated anyone who wasn't my color, and I was a bully all of a sudden."

"Sometimes when the kids single out a person and they start making fun of him, at first I object and I don't take part in it. But then, after a while, I start thinking like them and I laugh, too. Prejudice is sort of contagious."

Prejudice *is* contagious. When people are afraid or have actually been hurt, it may be a natural response to want to hurt back. But hurting one another only escalates the hatred and violence — and the differences don't go away. We live in a world of differences — different races, religions, cultures, sexual orientations, abilities. The differences can seem strange and overwhelming, even frightening. In an effort to cope, we may all find ourselves wanting just to stay with "our own kind," avoiding people who aren't like us, sometimes resorting to hurtful words and actions ourselves to manage our fears. At the beginning of this new century and millennium, we must deal with our differences — in schools and workplaces, in books and newspapers, on television and online, even in our own families.

Prejudice is only one way of dealing with differences. Instead, we can learn to respect differences, to

Current U.S. Population Statistics — 1990

TOTAL POPULATION: 248.7 MILLION

White	**80.3% (199.7 million)**
African-American	**12.1% (30.0 million)**
American Indian,	
Eskimo, or Aleut	**0.7% (1.7 million)**
Asian, Pacific Islander	**2.7% (6.6 million)**
Others	**2.1% (5.2 million)**
Women	**53% (126.1 million)**
People over 65 years	
of age	**12.5% (31.2 million)**
People with disabilities	**10% (24.6 million — estimate)**

see them as a source of strength in our lives and society, even celebrate them. In place of prejudice, we can teach acceptance and understanding. Meeting this challenge requires both preparation and practice.

Projects such as ADL's A WORLD OF DIFFERENCE® Institute have offered training and materials to hundreds of thousands of educators, thus reaching millions of students. As parents, we must reinforce their message — we must bring it home to our dinner tables and be sure that our children understand it.

This book offers you, as the primary influences in your children's lives, basic principles, skills, and strategies, along with real-life scenarios, to help you teach them to turn the fear and pain of prejudice into the courage and cooperation of understanding and respect.

In Part One, we will show you how children perceive differences at successive stages of their development. Our natural individual differences tend to become generalized into stereotypes of group differences. We explain how we can help ourselves and our children appreciate differences and resist forming biases about them. We offer guidance that can prevent differences from causing us to hurt or hate one another.

In Part Two, we give you true stories about children of different ages and backgrounds. The kids have been either the objects or the perpetrators of hateful words and actions, or they have observed or challenged hate directed at someone else. Here we offer specific advice on how to respond when your children face similar situations. Whatever role your child has played, you'll find helpful suggestions.

In Part Three, we provide guidelines for challenging and resisting biased material and information in schools, books, movies, on television, and online.

At the end of the book is a list of resources, including organizations and Web sites, reference books, and age-appropriate children's books, to aid you in continuing your efforts to close the book on hate.

"Not in Our Town"

On the night of December 2nd [1993] Tammy Schnitzer left her two children with a Vietnamese babysitter so she could attend a community meeting. When she returned, she drove the babysitter home.

"She could barely speak English, and yet she distinctly made out the words 'broken glass,'" Schnitzer recalled. "She kept saying something about 'broken glass' or 'glass broke.'"

Schnitzer returned home to find [her husband] Brian in tears as he sat on a rocking chair in the kitchen, holding [their son] Isaac.

"Why is it so cold in here?" she asked. She turned to find Isaac's room, where they had placed a menorah, a mess of broken glass and windswept linen. On the bed, amid the splintered shards, lay a cinder block.

"For the first time in my life, I felt like running, moving out," she said.

She called Schile at the *Billings Gazette*. Arguing over whether or not to run it as a front-page story, Schile suggested the publicity might further harm the Schnitzers.

"I told him I have no place else to go and I can't be afraid," she said.

Splayed across the front page of Montana's largest newspaper the next day was the bedroom, with Isaac standing behind the broken window.

Soon a host of local churches began instructing their Sunday school students to draw menorahs.

Four days after the incident, Schile printed a large black-and-white menorah on the back page of the *Gazette* and, in a front-page editorial, urged residents of Billings to display it in their windows. The symbol began appearing in hundreds of homes and businesses across the city.

This provoked the anti-Semitic activists. Eight more homes with menorahs were attacked.

Emboldened, thousands of Billings residents then placed menorahs in their windows. Hundreds of stores followed suit. Meanwhile, the association of churches began a drive to repair the [previously] vandalized black community's church. . . . Billboards proclaimed, "No Hate. No Violence."

The effort worked. Police Chief [Wayne] Inman reported a decrease in hate crimes in the weeks following the vigil. . . .

Part One

Understanding Hate and Where It Comes From

CHAPTER 1

From Birth to Teens: How Children Learn About Differences

"YOU'VE GOT TO BE CAREFULLY TAUGHT"

You've got to be taught to hate and fear.
You've got to be taught from year to year.
It's got to be drummed in your dear little ear.
You've got to be carefully taught.
You've got to be taught to be afraid
Of people whose eyes are oddly made,
And people whose skin is a diff'rent shade,
You've got to be carefully taught.
You've got to be taught before it's too late,
Before you are six or seven or eight,
To hate all the people your relatives hate!
You've got to be carefully taught!
You've got to be carefully taught!

> — song from the Broadway musical
> *South Pacific.* Copyright © 1949
> (Renewed) by Richard Rodgers
> and Oscar Hammerstein II.

All children notice differences. An infant hearing a new voice looks in the direction it came from. An eighteen-month-old knows that the toy you give him when he cries is not the same one he just dropped and wants back. A toddler knows that the green cup, not the blue cup, is "mine." A four-year-old knows that peanut butter, which she loves, is not tuna fish.

All of us are born with the ability to identify differences in our environments. As we grow, we learn to classify the differences in everything we perceive — sounds, colors, shapes, sizes. So children naturally notice that people come in all different shapes and sizes and colors. Noticing differences is biological. Forming attitudes about them is social. The good news is that we can shape how children value the differences they perceive.

Infants — I Distinguish Between "Me" and Others

From birth, each of us is different. Babies respond differently to their environments. One infant might be calm and contemplative; another might be more active, cry more loudly when hungry, and react more sensitively when the telephone rings or the bedside light goes on. Each one will want to eat and sleep at different times.

And all babies have the inborn gift to form relationships with other people. They smile when they're content, make eye contact with those who are caring for them, and coo back to the voices around them. And they learn that others respond to them when, for example, they get loving looks, smiles, and sweet talk in return.

In this early process of forming relationships, babies learn that the people around them are different. The crucial first lesson is the difference between "me" and others, an important step to understanding their own individuality. As long as infants can depend on their parents and caregivers to be responsive to their needs, they have a sense of security on which to base their developing identity. Once that basic sense of "self" is learned, babies then learn the differences among others.

First Discovery of "Others"

We can see clearly in the "relationships" babies form that they distinguish differences. But they don't make cultural assumptions to go along with them:

"Ben and Jennifer started at the child care center at four months of age and were assigned the same primary caregiver. Ben was quiet and calm, unaffected by sudden occurrences, and gracious about waiting to be fed. Jennifer was his opposite. Jen was tight-bodied and highly sensitive to changes in her environment. She cried loudly and persistently when hungry, sleepy, or upset. Their caregiver, Teresa, and respective family members saw that after only a month together, at five months of age, Ben and Jen were fascinated by each other. One would light up when the other arrived — Ben, smil-

**ing and opening his eyes wide with anticipa-
tion; Jennifer, wiggling every part of her
body, making high-pitched sounds. Lying on
their tummies and looking at each other was
a favorite activity. Both would arch their
backs and heads until they could hold them
up no more, then collapse. When one was
facedown, the other would use body and
voice to summon the partner back."**

Ben is "quiet and calm . . . gracious," traits that
often get labeled as "female." Jen, on the other
hand, is "tight-bodied" and "loud," more like the
adult stereotype of "male." And yet at this stage,
they simply like each other and find their natural
differences a source of mutual interest and attrac-
tion.

The differences among us are complementary if
we will just follow our natural constructs, not our social ones. From infancy, we are inquisitive and
drawn to others with traits unlike our own.

At **six months,** infants are gaining better motor
control. They can hold their heads steadier, roll over,
even begin to sit up. When a six-month-old makes
eye contact with another person, then turns away
and nuzzles his face into his mother's shoulder, he is

doing his first "hiding." He is beginning to understand that he is a separate person. And he can also see more clearly the differences and separateness of others.

Children can also distinguish different skin colors, hair textures, and facial features from as early as six months of age. In an experiment conducted by Dr. Phyllis Katz at the Institute for Research on Social Problems, located in Boulder, Colorado, an infant shown a series of pictures of faces of the same color grew bored and inattentive. When a face of a different color was introduced, the infant noticed and became interested again. Dr. Katz has concluded from the results of such experiments that "children are already using [race] in some rudimentary way at six months." It seems likely that babies at this stage instinctively enjoy and appreciate differences. And differences help babies form a secure knowledge of themselves as entities separate from others.

> **" Children are already using [race] in some rudimentary way at six months. "**

Toddlers — I Explore Differences

Between **eight** and **eighteen months,** children make the transition from infant to toddler. They learn to sit up, crawl, and climb. Now they are able to explore their environment by moving themselves around in it. And they learn that the people in the environment can even go away. That's why peekaboo and hide-and-seek are often favorite games at this stage, but also why children at this age don't like it when Mommy leaves the room or get frightened when unfamiliar people approach. Attachment and separation become the primary issues at this stage as kids continue their discovery of their own individuality.

They start to recognize their own features in others. They begin to identify with people who look like they do. They imitate the activities and behavior of the loved adults in their lives. A child given a choice of playing with a doll of

> **A child given a choice of playing with a doll of his or her own color or a different color will often choose the doll of his or her own color.**

his or her own color or a different color will often choose the doll of his or her own color. This apparent preference is not necessarily an early sign of prejudice; it may simply show the infant's developing ability to distinguish between differences and similarities as he or she begins to build a healthy self-image.

First Questions About Differences

As they reach the age of **two**, children continue to be increasingly aware of the physical aspects of identity, especially gender. They are very interested in the differences between boys' and girls' bodies, and since they're usually talking at this age, they can begin to ask questions. The toilet training that goes on at this stage offers plenty of opportunities for curiosity and clarification. ("Why does Andy stand up to pee?" "Why does Janelle sit down?") They also want to know what "rules" apply to each gender. ("Is pink just a girl color?" "Do only boys play with trucks?")

Awareness of other physical differences, such as the inability to walk or hear or see, follows close behind gender differences. Two- to three-year-olds also begin to notice that some people eat different foods ("What are tortillas?") or do things differently ("Why aren't they eating anything?" "What is Ramadan?").

If they are part of a diverse environment or regularly exposed to a broad range of people, and the adults in their lives answer their questions directly and honestly, kids at this age are usually interested in and open to differences:

"Mommy, what's that man riding in?"

"That's a wheelchair."

"Why don't I get to ride in a wheelchair?"

"Wheelchairs are for people who have trouble walking."

"Like I used to ride in a stroller?"

Three- to Five-Year-Olds — I'm Learning to Interact with Others

Motor skills and sense of self continue to develop in children between the ages of three and five. For the first time, they begin to apply these developmental skills to the world beyond home or their place of care. Now they seek more sophisticated explanations for the differences they see.

Most **three-** and **four-year-olds** are still figuring out physical differences:

"Why don't I have the same color eyes as yours?"

"*Why* is my skin brown? Why is Lisa's a different color?"

"Will I change color when I grow up?"

"When I wear pants, am I a boy?"

Their perception of cultural differences lags behind. Their sense of their racial or cultural heritage hasn't been fully formed yet. When a preschool teacher asked a room full of three-year-olds of different religions "Who celebrates Chanukah?" all the children raised their hands, although most didn't even know what Chanukah was. Their natural instincts — especially if they are exposed to different kinds of people — may be to belong, regardless of differences that are obvious to adults.

Kids in this age group don't yet understand the cultural meanings of the labels society at large applies to people. They tend to see things literally, without attaching judgments. A "white" child with dark hair and a dark complexion may insist that she's black. A "black" child of lighter skin may say he's brown.

By **five,** many kids can begin to understand scientific explanations for differences in skin, hair, and eye color. They know they have a family history and traditions. They begin to build a group ethnic identity to go along with their personal identity. Children in this age group identify with similarities in others as they construct their self-image and understand their heritage. Now they learn what holidays mean. They may be more inquisitive about the range of differences within and between racial and ethnic groups. ("Why don't we have a Christmas tree?" "Why don't we celebrate Kwanza?")

Self-worth Develops

Between **three** and **five,** a child's self-image and
sense of worth also begin to stabilize. Healthy kids
are developing a stronger sense of their own individuality as well as a sense of how others perceive
them. They can compare themselves with others
now. They are increasingly social beings, able to
form real friendships with their peers.

**"Lourdes lives with her mother and sister in
a suburban community. When she starts
kindergarten, she is almost monolingual in
Spanish. She has excellent motor skills, both
large and fine, and excels at almost any
physical activity she tries.**

**"Lourdes shows artistic ability, producing
detailed drawings and paintings at an early
age. She loves to dress and undress dolls. She
has an affinity for music and learned to play
the piano with ease.**

**"In her first year at school, Lourdes strug-
gles to learn English and make friends. She
can sometimes be clumsy in approaching
other children, so her mother coaches her on
what to do and say to help other people get**

to like her. Together they rejoice when she receives her first birthday party invitation."

Lourdes's mother is an excellent coach. Teaching her to go up to other children and express interest in them gives Lourdes the self-confidence to make friends. By encouraging her to do so without waiting to be approached first, to share her Spanish delicacies with others at lunch, and to help them pronounce words such as *tortilla* and *churro*, she has given her a valuable early lesson in socializing across cultural lines.

Children Are Not Color-blind

At this age, kids may also begin to show signs that they are developing negative attitudes toward difference. In another experiment conducted by Dr. Katz, a three-year-old white girl, Morgan, from an all-white preschool in Denver, is asked questions by a white female "tester" about racial difference:

"What are white people like?"

"Me."

"What are black people like?"

"Like somebody else."

"Are they just like other people except for their color?"

Morgan shakes her head no.

Next, Morgan sits in a darkened room with the tester and looks at slides, each showing a black child and a white child. When a slide of two school-age girls comes on the screen, the tester says, "One of these girls is really good at school. She does all of her work and she gets it all right. Which one of these girls is the one who does everything right?" Morgan gets up and goes to the screen and points to the white girl. "How come you think that's the one?" asks the tester. "'Cause she's white," answers Morgan.

For the next slide, showing two boys, the tester asks Morgan which one threw trash on the floor. Morgan gets up and points to the black boy.

Between the ages of three and five, children learn group identities and then naively accept the values placed on various groups by those in their close-knit world. Unfortunately, that world today in-cludes not only family and friends of family and caregivers, it also includes the media — television, radio, recorded music, picture books, even the Inter-net. Parents of children Morgan's age are often sur-prised to learn that their kids have acquired such values and wonder what has influenced them. As one mother in Denver put it, "It's something I thought he didn't notice . . . that wouldn't be part of his consciousness. I don't *want* it to be part of his consciousness. . . . I sort of wanted him to be color-blind." Clearly, children are NOT color-blind. Unless they are taught to appreciate differences, their views, like Morgan's, can be color-coded in a very negative way quite early.

This is also the stage in which kids who have found that others have biased attitudes toward them may begin to internalize these attitudes. In the same Katz experiment, a black female tester shows Jason, a young black boy, a slide of a white boy and a black boy playing chess. When she asks, "Which one is going to win?" he answers, "The black boy's not going to win. He doesn't want to win."

Jason has already absorbed negative perceptions of black men in forming his group identity, and he has accepted the idea that the motivation to win at intellectual activity, let alone winning itself, is not consistent with black males. What would have been Jason's likely response had he been shown the two boys playing basketball?

This is obviously an age when the perception of

difference can start to be externalized as prejudice or internalized as self-hatred. When parents and other important adults in a child's life see signs of discomfort, fear, or avoidance of people who are different, or signs that a child considers himself unworthy, there are steps that can be taken to turn those feelings back into an appreciation of differences and a strong sense of self-worth. The first step is to notice these feelings in children. In Chapter 4, we will give you detailed strategies and skills for helping overcome them.

Six- to Eight-Year-Olds — I'm Myself and I'm Part of Society

Between the ages of **six** and **eight,** kids are starting their primary school education. For some, it's the first time they've been fully exposed to the world outside their family and their neighborhood. It's a time of tremendous growth — cognitively, emotionally, socially, morally. They learn to read and write, allowing them to extend their knowledge beyond the things they see and hear. With access to a wealth of other views, they start to compare and express their own.

They've learned that they are either boys or girls, regardless of what they wear or whether they prefer playing sports to playing with dolls. They've learned that their eye and skin colors are not going to change as they grow up. They have a fuller understanding of their heritage and ethnicity and that of others. ("We don't have a Christmas tree because we're Jewish." "We don't observe Ramadan because Mommy and Daddy are Buddhist.")

They have a more developed sense of their self-image and self-worth, which now becomes harder for them to change. They have a more flexible sense of the "rules" that apply to behavior but are increasingly aware of social and cultural expectations. They are beginning to have a larger sense of history and human diversity.

First Conscious Contact with Hate

his is also the stage at which many kids — of all different backgrounds — report their initial conscious encounters with racism and other kinds of prejudice. As they enter the "mainstream" of society, they may find themselves without the knowledge or skills to deal with "others." They have to deal with the negative attitudes that others have about them and to address issues of belonging. Some children find themselves being called hurtful names, excluded from activities, isolated, even threatened or attacked.

If these kids felt "less than" before they started elementary school, those feelings may become more acute. Other children may for the first time act out attitudes like Morgan's, which are expressed as name-calling, exclusion, pretension, or aggression.

Four groups of elementary school kids in the Minneapolis–Saint Paul area — one black, one Chinese, one Native American, and one white — shared their experiences with prejudice:

A sixth grader said that from first grade on,

classmates called her names. "One hint of black and they call you nigger. (Her father is white; her mother is black.) They say, 'All of them look the same.' It hurts so much you just want to rip all your skin off and jump into a new one. . . . You wish you were never that color and never born some- times."

> **It hurts so much you just want to rip all your skin off and jump into a new one. . . . You wish you were never that color and never born sometimes.**

A Native American boy said he and his friends were called "savages." "What do you think you can do about people who call you names?" asked the reporter. "Tell them I want to make friends." "You want to make friends with people who make fun of you?" The boy nodded. "Have you tried?" The boy nodded again. "What happened?" "They tried to beat me up."

A boy of Hmong ancestry said, "Black people call me chink, so I call them nigger back." "Do you mean it?" asked the reporter. "I don't mean it — I just try to get them away from me." "Why do you think they call you names?" "[Because] this is not Hmong country."

A white child heard this said about her: "I don't

want to play with her, she's white." Another was told, "Get off me, white honky. I just hate white people."

The kids in all the groups seemed to agree that "It's just easier to relate to people of your own race," that it wasn't possible to combat the prejudices they felt and experienced.

From Hate to Hope

But it *is* possible. Kids of this age group look to parents and other adults they admire for hope, guidance, and approval. One of their primary motivations in learning at this stage is to master the skills and follow the examples of the adults around them. If parents and caregivers talk to children about prejudice, stand up to words and acts of discrimination they encounter themselves, and model other ways of resolving conflict, children can learn to do the same.

Had the parents, teachers, and counselors of those kids known the proper responses and taught them to the kids, they would have been more hopeful. There isn't a happy ending to every hateful situation. But it is possible to preserve a child's sense of self-worth and optimism despite such encounters.

An ADL facilitator recalled this story:

"Every day on this child's route home, he passed the home of a popular player on his school's football team. The athlete always called out racial slurs to him. The child tried everything reasonable, from calmly letting the kid know his remarks were hurtful and unacceptable, to crossing the street out of easy earshot, to telling the school authorities, who could do nothing since it was not occurring on the premises or at a school function. Finally, there was nothing to do but ignore the big guy's comments. Yet this child came to understand that this person's words were no reflection on him at all and learned not to judge other individuals based on this one person's actions."

Although we can't always change the attitudes or behavior of others, we can learn that one person's hurtful words and actions need not label us — or lead us to label others who are "like" him.

Nine- to Twelve-Year-Olds — Myself, My World, My Own Values

B etween the ages of **nine** and **twelve**, kids are gaining a greater understanding of how history and geography shape various aspects of culture. They can now understand what racial and cultural stereotypes, prejudice, and discrimination mean and how these things affect what people say and do, as well as how they live. They begin to establish their own concepts of "right" and "wrong."

If their experience of differences has been positive, they will more readily accept differences as something to be valued. If their experience of differences is negative, they will likely become biased.

And yet biased attitudes at this stage can be "un-learned." The kids we quoted in the opening of this book attended a workshop conducted at I.S. 70 in Manhattan that was sponsored by the Board of Education and the Peace Education Program for preteens who had been selected as potential leaders. It demonstrated the possibility of turning attitudes around. Unlike the elementary school kids in the report from Minneapolis, the I.S. 70 kids of all races and backgrounds — Chinese, Korean, African, Hispanic, white, and African-American — sat together in the same room. They shared the experiences they'd had with prejudice, both their own and that of others toward them. Together, through discussion and role-playing, they learned to acknowledge their own pain, to face their own mistakes, and to stand up for others who are the victims of hurtful words and acts. These are just a few of many examples of youths standing up to prejudice:

"He was calling me names like 'ching-chong.' And I was just mad he could say anything like that to anybody [and I told him so]. He called me up that night and told me he was sorry he hurt my feelings. And I felt really good."

"I had a conversation yesterday with the crippled guy I used to tease. . . . I realized I was the one who was wrong. That's where I got the courage to face my problem."

"I was with some relative of mine. We were walking down the street and saw a black guy

coming. My relative said something, and I said, 'You shouldn't be afraid that you're gonna get mugged by a black person. Anyone can mug you — not just a black person.'"

Instead of concluding that "It's just easier to relate to people of your own race," they learned to see beyond their differences and confront biased attitudes in themselves and their peers.

At the end of the week-long workshop, they all shared their own first impressions of one another and told how they had changed: "Now that I got to know you, I see that you're not what I thought. You're a nice person." As a reporter on the project commented, "Now there is a chance for, if not friendship, at least a lot more understanding."

Teenagers — I'm Independent, Except When I Need You

Teenagers are on the verge of adulthood, struggling constantly with their need for dependence versus their desire for independence. Among themselves, inclusive and exclusive behavior may reach its lifetime peak and may show elements of prejudice against those who are different from themselves, however unconscious. ("Oh, that was sooo gay!" "That was really lame.") At the same time, teens are acutely sensitive to hypocrisy on the part of the adults in their lives.

As a parent, you may find *yourself* more frequently the target of hurtful remarks at this stage, with many of your own behaviors and beliefs challenged.

"I told you to clean up your room."

"Why should I? It's my room. I like it messy."

"But it's my house, and you'll do what I say."

"I'm getting worried that your friend Jay is a bad influence."

"You don't even know him."

"Well, if you brought him home, I'd get to know him."

"Why would he want to come here, when you don't like him? It's my life, and I'll hang out with whoever I want."

Such exchanges are all too familiar to parents of
a teenager. That sweet little boy who used to cry
when we went away and wanted us to come see him
play on the soccer team, or that affectionate little
girl who used to tell us everything and beg us for
another book at storytime is now half-child, half-
adult antagonist. Teens arrive at sexual maturity
before social maturity and are critical of the primary adults in their lives. They demand freedom on
the one hand and refuse to take responsibility on
the other. Eager for role models, they can be ruthless
in their judgment of who deserves the title.

Cruelty May *Not* Be Hate

In their efforts to find their place in the adult world,
teenagers can also be enormously cruel to one another. It can be especially hard to separate and address all the issues — prejudice among them — that
emerge as teens take important steps to achieving
the wholeness of their adult individuality. The con-
stant push and pull that earmarks a teenager's emotional development makes it difficult to determine
what strategy will work with your teen at any given
moment. But there *are* strategies that will help you
and your teenager navigate the crucial passage of

these years into the grown-up world of difference. Just listening becomes very important at this stage, when a teenager is trying to establish his own point of view but still wants guidance, whether he can admit it or not.

Parents of teenagers in our society must learn to listen to what their offspring are saying, especially what they are saying to one another. That can only happen by developing relationships in which parents are available without forcing themselves on their children. Plan activities they enjoy that you can participate in together. Accompany them to important events. Learn about and follow their interests. Get to know their friends and the families of their friends. But be careful not to "pry" — otherwise, you may find your teenager becoming closed and secretive.

> **"Parents of teenagers in our society must learn to listen to what their offspring are saying, especially what they are saying to one another."**

Understanding the difference between secrecy and privacy is essential in developing good communication with teens, as is the ability to confront issues in a way that enables young people to disclose information and receive correction without perceiving condemnation. Be prepared for teenagers to claim that correction and condemnation are the same — and seem to reject both — but know that teens internally experience these actions very differently, and that they really do hear what we say.

Teenagers need to be allowed to voice their biases. Sensitive adults will listen without expressing shock or condemnation of the individual teen, respecting the youth's desire for independent thinking. Encouraging teens to talk freely about the circumstances and events in their lives that have given voice to the bias will go a long way toward reshaping values. Parents may happily discover that the issue really is jealousy, cliques, personality conflicts, or any of the other myriad issues teens are learning to handle. In any case, modeling the behavior, living the values, and repeatedly speaking the concepts you want teens to adopt are the surest ways to help teenagers learn to understand and cherish the differences among us.

Conclusion

From the infant's first sensory perceptions, to the toddler's tentative explorations, to the two- and three-year-old's charming questions, to the first grader's early classroom experiences, through the tumult of the teens, the road to individual development is paved with differences. How a child learns to deal with differences depends largely on how parents, caregivers, and other important adults deal with differences. It also depends on the child's experiences.

It is important to understand your child's needs at each age in order to shape values that appreciate differences and to choose environments that will expose your child to a wide variety of individuals. Teaching a child understanding and appreciation of others is not easy even when the others are "like" himself. It is truly a challenge when the others are "different" from him. But just as participating in the growth of children is filled with an almost inconceivable number of rewards and joys, so, too, is helping them grow into respectful adults who genuinely respect and value individuals based on their human worth, regardless of social categories.

In the next chapter we will discuss the development of these social classifications of differences — gender, sexual orientation, race, religion, culture and ethnicity orientation — and learn that they are simply social constructs, ones we can deconstruct for ourselves and our children.

> **Train a child in the way he should go, and when he is old he will not turn from it.**
> **Proverbs 22:6**
> **NIV**

CHAPTER 2

Some Things That Make People Different From One Another

O nce we understand how our children learn about differences, our goal is to influence their learning. We want to help our children feel good about who and what they are so that when others perceive them as "different" their self-images remain healthy. We also want to teach them to place a high value on diversity. Despite these good intentions, we are often left without meaningful explanations to give our children. We often do not have a solid understanding of the various "differences."

Gender

natomical differences are obvious even to toddlers. While they may not yet associate specific behaviors with genders, toddlers are indeed aware of "who has a what and who doesn't." Often their first experience with diversity is framed by the question, "Am I a girl or a boy?" It is their first search for answers to the questions: "Who am I? What am I? How do I feel about it?"

Although American society has taken huge steps toward gender equity, the reality is that many gender stereotypes still prevail. While we might intellectually believe that a job can be done equally well by either a man or a woman, many of us were raised with subtle (and at times not so subtle) messages about what it means to be either a girl or a boy. Perhaps we learned:

◆ Girls are compassionate and gentle.

◆ Boys are strong.

◆ Girls are more nurturing.

◆ Boys are more naturally athletic.

◆   Girls don't hit.

◆   Boys don't cry.

And so on. We may not consciously act on these beliefs, yet they do pervade our behaviors and attitudes.

This point was driven home at a recent diversity training program conducted for parents. The facilitator began his program by asking the group to yell out an answer to the fill-in-the-blank statement he was about to make. He then said, "The moon is made of _____." Unanimously, the fifty adults in the room yelled out "CHEESE." How often do we refer to instinctive responses — ones we *know* are not based on truth — in our day-to-day interactions with our children?

Write a list of the gender-specific stereotypes that you were told, became aware of, or broke through as you were growing up. Include ones you still experience today. If you have a partner in raising your children, ask him or her to do the same. Ask yourselves such questions as:

◆   What roles do you associate with your gender identity?

◆ How did you learn these roles?

◆ What interests and/or activities have you decided not to pursue because they seemed inappropriate for your gender?

Compare your responses and talk about how these statements have had an impact on each of you. Next, consider:

◆ What messages do you think you have already sent your children about their gender identity?

◆ What messages would you like to send? Are you comfortable when Jane seeks out a truck to play with? Or when Johnny insists on owning his very own Barbie™ doll? Do you introduce these options? Have you established a double standard for your sons and daughters when it comes to curfews, household chores, holding a job, getting dressed up, dating, and so forth?

Bearing in mind that gender is the first acknowledgment of the many differences that exist among people, how you handle this difference can set the stage for how your children react to future differences. It is important to help your children feel good about this difference. Do not leave it to chance. Instead, make a point of exposing them to both male and female role models. Ensure that they are aware that both men and women have significantly contributed to the success of our nation. And be sure to point out that these contributions have crossed all fields. Encourage younger children to seek out heroes of both genders.

As you go through this process, consider the age and maturity of your children. Just as the toddler may ask "Am I boy or a girl?" preschoolers will begin to form assumptions about what these designations mean. They want to know the "rules" for being boys and girls. Questions such as "Are the flowered ones 'girl' lunch boxes?" often are meant to assist them in establishing these rules. By elementary school, kids have integrated their gender into their initial sense of self. This usually leads them to practice their roles with peers of the same sex. ("Tiffany, Jodie, Kate, Aisha, and I are best friends for life, forever, just us five." "Jamie, Chad, Jamal, and I are a crew — no girls allowed.")

By junior high school, children begin to test their sexuality on their way to adult relationships.

Sexual Orientation

As children arrive at puberty, questions about sexual orientation may also arise. Because most adults are uncomfortable discussing even the basic "birds and bees" with their children, branching into a discussion of sexual orientation is often a very difficult task. Like the knee-jerk reaction some have to the idea that the moon is made of cheese, many hold unconscious beliefs in myths and stereotypes about people who are not heterosexual. Such internalized misconceptions lead to homophobia, an irrational fear of gay, lesbian, and bisexual people.

The words associated with sexual orientation are widely used in our culture and may enter the vocabulary of our children long before their meaning is understood. As one dad described:

"I picked up my seven-year-old and my ten-year-old from sleep-away camp and began the long drive home. For the first hour they got along well as they began to tell stories about their camp experiences. However, by

the third hour, they were at each other's throats. Much to my surprise, I heard my seven-year-old call his sister a lesbian. I asked him if he knew what the word meant.

" 'Yes,' he replied, 'a lesbian is when a girl has sex with another girl.' A few minutes went by as I struggled with finding a response to the obvious sex education he had gotten over the summer.

" 'And,' he added, 'you know, Dad, when a guy has sex with another guy, well, then he's gay.'

"I stared at my seven-year-old and was about to launch into one of my best 'dad speeches' when he concluded by asking, 'Hey, Dad, what is sex anyway?' "

Always listen to find out what your child is asking, as well as why the question is being posed, before you respond. Here the child had the words without the understanding or experience to make sense of them. But at some point he — like all of us — will knowingly or unknowingly have gay, lesbian, or bisexual colleagues, friends, or relatives. Or he may discover he is gay himself. And without a doubt, he will be exposed to the homophobic behavior of others.

People who are gay, lesbian, or bisexual are among the most frequent targets of hate crimes. We know that the best antidote to hate is education. Even if you find this a difficult topic to address, why would you leave the responsibility for inoculating your child against this type of hate to someone other than yourself?

If gay, lesbian, or bisexual activity contradicts your religious beliefs, consider how you deal with people who may depart from your beliefs because they practice a different faith, have been divorced, participate in premarital sex, don't keep kosher, eat meat on fast days during Lent, etc. Most adults understand in these cases that they can treat someone with respect and dignity even if they do not condone all aspects of the way that person lives.

Some adults find jokes or derogatory comments about gay, lesbian, and bisexual people in some way more acceptable than comments or jokes based on race, religious beliefs and practices, abilities, etc. But they are just as hurtful. Ask yourself if it is any less hateful to accept and laugh at stereotypes about people who are gay than about people of a particular race, religion, or culture. The answer is simply "no."

The difficulty a young person faces in accepting that he or she is gay, lesbian, or bisexual and telling others makes it all the more important to have a proactive rather than a responsive conversation.

"Growing up with the feeling that you might be gay is a unique experience. While people with racial or religious differences often find themselves victimized because of their differences, when they are the targets of bigotry they usually can find comfort and safety with their friends and family. On the other hand, a gay teenager cannot count on this support. Instead of support, young gay people often face rejection from the very people who are supposed to love them.

"This was the case for me. My mother said terrible things about gay people — how they were dirty, disgusting, sick perverts with whom she would not associate. All the while she didn't know that I was one of those 'horrible' creatures that she was describing. I felt less than human."

Unfortunately, in our work at ADL we have heard this same story more times than you can

> **One does not choose to be male or female. Neither is sexual orientation a matter of choice.**

imagine. One does not choose to be male or female. Neither is sexual orientation a matter of choice. You are not being asked to approve or disapprove of a particular sexual orientation. Your role is to help your child understand that a person's sexual orientation does not legitimize hateful behavior or disrespect and does not preclude positive self-image and self-respect.

In talking with your children, help them understand the nature of "hate" that many gay, lesbian, and bisexual people face. They are often forced or frightened into keeping their full identity hidden, even from family and friends. Having to keep their sexual orientation a secret can make them feel alone, ashamed, guilty, and ultimately depressed. Statistics have shown the suicide rate for gay, lesbian, or bisexual teenagers is dramatically high. For no other reason than this, we cannot let embarrassment, religious beliefs, or homophobia be an excuse for avoiding this discussion.

Often, those who have great difficulty in dealing with this issue discover that their feelings change after they learn that someone they love is affected by their view of this difference:

"When I did finally have the conversation that I had dreaded my entire life, [my mother's] initial reaction surprised me. Instead of being angry, she started to cry. She said that she was upset because she was worried about me. She said that she was afraid of people hurting me or rejecting me because I was gay. I explained that she was the one who had been hurting me with all the negative things she had said about gay people while I was growing up.

"My mom took the next few years to educate herself about gay people. . . . She asked me a ton of questions and read several reputable books about gay people. Just as it had taken me a long time to understand and eventually love what it means to be a gay person, she needed time to learn and grow. Now, eleven years later, all is forgiven. Knowing that . . . she fully supports and appreciates me has drawn us very close as mother and son."

Being open and honest with themselves, their friends, and their families is both a relief and a positive experience for most gay, lesbian, and bisexual teenagers. What parent would not want to help his or her child feel better about himself or herself?

Race

"Growing up in . . . the early fifties meant that I got to see certain movie theaters that had traditionally admitted only whites forced to open their doors to everyone. When I was twelve years old, dressed in the new outfit I had worn for Easter and feeling very pretty, I took the streetcar by myself to the theater downtown. Just before it was time for the theater to open, an usher came out and asked us to all form a line. People just kind of merged together. . . . Suddenly, I heard a group of women in back of me talking: 'This little darkie wasn't in front of us. She doesn't belong here. With that, I was thrown out of line. I started to cry. . . . I had never been called a darkie before and I couldn't recall ever being treated so meanly.

"By the time I got home, I was feeling pretty miserable. I couldn't understand why I had been called that name. My mom had me sit very close to her and she put her hand on my shoulder. She said, 'Sometimes people who don't know other people who look different from them just decide to dislike them. This action is called prejudice. . . . It is wrong to form an opinion of someone based solely on what you see. You must try to get to know the person before you say whether you like him or her. Certainly the color of one's skin has nothing to do with what's in one's heart. I know you feel hurt, but you must not hate. Hate is not good for anyone. Remember to take a journey. Try to see as far as you can into a person's heart to see all of the good that you can.'"

One can almost believe that "we've come a long way" toward eradicating racism since the 1950s. That is, until your own child comes home crying because she was called a _____. When your child is on the receiving end of hate, all the progress in the world doesn't matter. How do you explain to the children you love why others mistreat them?

The oldest definition of race is "generation" or "the act of producing offspring." It came to mean "the descendants of a common ancestor: a family, tribe, people, or nation belonging to the same stock." Today, most people use the term race to classify people who share certain physical characteristics such as skin color, hair texture, and eye shape. And, as with most classifications, people often incorrectly associate personal qualities and behaviors with specific racial classifications.

Helping our children understand racial differences demands that we meet three challenges:

1. Assist them in their own self-definition in answering "Who am I?" and "What am I?"

2. Ensure that they are proud of who and what they are without feeling superior or relegating others to an inferior status.

3. Help them see that people are unique, that we cannot draw general conclusions about people based on physical characteristics.

The first step in the process is to look at yourself. While no one is born a bigot, by the time we are adults most of us have developed some prejudices. While we may feel very relaxed about working with people who are different from us, perhaps we are not as comfortable about living in a mixed environment or in one in which we find ourselves in the minority. Some of us may be perfectly happy that our children have friends of all backgrounds as long as they only date people who we see as the same as our family.

Others of us perhaps preach integration and praise the differences that exist among various people but fail to practice what we preach. We only expose our children to one type of art, one type of music. Or we only invite people who are different from ourselves into our homes when they are hired to perform a task. What

> **What signals are our words and actions sending our children?**

signals are our words and actions sending our children? Consider the messages you received as a child and ask yourself how they have an impact on the ones you are sending.

Be prepared to acknowledge that you, too, are working on your prejudices. Think about how you define yourself. How do you answer the questions "Who am I? What am I?" How do you feel about those descriptions? Can you articulate those feelings?

Find two or three people to do the following exercise with you. Allow at least a half hour to complete the exercise (longer if you are more than three people). Sit comfortably, and after a few minutes of thought, have each person complete each of the following four sentences:

1.   If I had to describe myself in terms of my heritage in four words or less, I would say I was a

——————, ——————, ——————, ——————.

2.   One time in which I was really aware that I was at least one of those four words was:

_____.

3.   One thing that makes me feel really proud about being each of those four words is:

_____.

4.   One thing that is difficult or embarrassing about being one or each of those four words is:

_____.

Not only will the exercise help you find the words to describe yourself to your children, it will help you remember what it was like to seek to define yourself and how you feel about your answers.

The second step is actually planning a conversation with your children before they witness racism or, even worse, fall victim to it. Challenge your children to begin the process of examining how they see themselves. Share your own self-perceptions as well as your self-exploration process. Discuss their inherited physical characteristics and racial origins. Provide your children with information that will help them see this information in a positive light.

The conversation cannot end with self-exploration. You must also prepare your children for the reality of what may exist outside your home. Take time to explain that prejudice and discrimination may be blatant, but more often than not, subtle. Frequently, the victims are left wondering if they really experienced it or are just jumping to conclusions. Make sure kids understand that subtle racism can be just as painful as the blatant kind. One way to make this point is to compare it to a well-known physics fact. If you pour a bucket of water on a brick, you will have a brick that is obviously wet. You can show it to someone and prove that it is wet without argument. If instead you drip tiny but consistent drops of water on the same place on the brick, it will eventually break into pieces. The same happens with subtle racism. If the drops are delivered consistently, people are worn away and some even break because of what may be perceived as a little drop of water. Invite your children to come to you to discuss what they are experiencing or seeing others experience. Share your experiences with them — let them know that you, too, are examining your biases and working to rid yourself of them.

Acknowledge that being viewed as "different" can be painful, but it can also be empowering and positive. Show your children examples of individuals who turned hatred and oppression into triumph and became stronger as a result. The same water that can crack a brick can cut stone into the unparalleled beauty of the Grand Canyon. Help them understand that hate hurts, but it doesn't have to break us. We can use it to mold ourselves into individuals of the highest caliber.

An important part of the conversation with your children must be a discussion of possible reactions. Practice possible responses, taking safety and reality into consideration. Help them identify allies — people they can turn to for support. During this discussion, if talking to very young children, be sure that they understand that just because someone is a "grown-up" does not mean he or she always knows what is best or is always right.

"I was about twelve years old when I first learned that someone I loved and respected could be wrong. My grandmother persisted in calling black people by an ugly name. I thought no one had told her people didn't use that name anymore. When I told her very politely and respectfully, 'Granny, you mean "black,"' she said, 'No, I mean _____.' I didn't say anything then, but that moment is seared in my brain as my revelation that grown-ups weren't ALWAYS right."

If we have been fortunate, we've had parents, teachers, religious leaders, or other adults who themselves interacted positively with people of different races. We've learned from them how to form relationships based on personal rather than racial qualities. Even if we haven't been so fortunate, we can still help our children by examining our own attitudes — including those we'd like to change — and honestly sharing them with our children.

Religion

Although we are usually born into a religion, in American society, religion ultimately comes down to choice. Our religious choices often reflect our most deeply held convictions about our place and purpose. Therefore, explaining religious differences to kids can be especially challenging. We want to reinforce our own faith, yet we want to instill a sense of respect for other faiths. We do not want to contradict ourselves, and we need to work hard not to compare or contrast different faiths in a way that creates competition.

Our children may at first be surprised to find out that religion is a difference at all, but their understanding of religious differences grows more sophisticated as they grow older:

"I remember one three-year-old I taught in my preschool class — James O'Reilly. We started to talk about the holidays and I mentioned that James was Catholic. He looked at me very surprised and said, 'I'm Catholic? I thought I was an O'Reilly! Can I be both?'"

Throughout our childhood, we want to belong to a group — to fit in. For preschoolers, who don't yet understand what makes religions different, a desire to celebrate every religious holiday, regardless of their own faith, is natural. Their instincts are to appreciate and want to participate in the whole range of our differences.

By elementary school, children begin to focus on what it means to belong to their own group, to distinguish their own religious beliefs and practices. This is not always an easy transition:

"All of the kids in my class were busy making tree ornaments for their Christmas trees. Since my teacher knew I was Jewish, she asked me to make a Happy Chanukah sign instead. It wasn't that my sign wasn't nice. I liked my sign. It's just that I felt so left out."

Most children will first encounter religious differences in the form of holiday practices long before they fully comprehend the reasons and beliefs that lead to them. Since the practices have no depth of meaning to them, they may not understand why they are asked not to participate or are excluded in

some way. Celebrations can be very enticing. Your
child will need more of an explanation than "We
just don't believe in that" if he or she is expected to
respectfully decline participation in another child's
religious ritual or celebration. Our children need to
know what we *do* believe and what our practices,
customs, and rituals are. They need to have opportunities to associate with others who share these beliefs and rituals. And they need to have a place
within them:

**"On Friday nights my mother always lit the
Sabbath candles. I remember the first time
she asked me to stand next to her as she ig-
nited the flames and chanted the blessings.
She pointed out that this was something she
had done with her mother and that she
hoped someday I would have a daughter to
stand by my side. She explained the meaning
of the candles — their role in welcoming the
Sabbath. After that, Friday nights always felt
so special."**

Helping our children feel connected to and
proud of our religions must include a respect for
those whose beliefs are different. Most books of

faith, from the Hebrew Bible to the Christian Bible to the Qur'an, teach in some fashion to "love your neighbor as you would yourself." A strong belief in our own religion should include respect for others.

We need to discuss our beliefs with our children and, to the extent that we are familiar with the beliefs of other faiths, those as well. Agree to work together to get the answers that you do not readily know to questions your child asks. Help your child learn respectful ways to ask questions of those whose practices he or she might not understand.

Unless you reside in a religious enclave, by high school your children will have experienced natural interfaith interactions. They will have witnessed different traditions and even participated in them. Interfaith exchanges usually produce understanding and an appreciation of our differences. The more knowledgeable your child is before the exchange, the better the experience will be. Talk about what to expect. Ensure that your child is able to answer basic questions about his or her own traditions or is supplied with a comfortable way to say, "I don't know, but I'll find out."

Even the most prepared child may emerge with ideas that are not positive. It is important that interfaith exchanges are followed by conversation. Ask what your child experienced: how it felt, what he enjoyed, what she didn't like, and why. Use this opportunity to negate any stereotypes or negative images that might arise.

Sometimes a religion-based action can be unintentionally misunderstood. Note the following situations:

"I saw the moving van arrive and the men begin to unload boxes into the house next door. When I saw a swing set, I thought, 'Great! They have kids!' as visions of play dates ran through my head. I awoke the next day to the sounds of hammering and sawing. Much to my chagrin I saw a seven-foot-tall fence going up around their backyard. I looked at the cake I had baked yesterday to bring to my new neighbor and decided that if they were fencing me out, I would eat it myself. It wasn't until weeks later that I learned that the woman of the house was an orthodox Muslim and that she had had the fence erected so that she could watch her daughters in the backyard without having to be veiled. What I took for unfriendliness was only misinterpreted religious practice."

"Not knowing the Buddhist funeral rituals, I assumed they would be the same as ours. Thus, I went out, bought a great deal of food, and headed for the home of the son of my friend who had passed away. I didn't know I was offending them by entering the house. I wish I had asked questions beforehand."

Help your children understand that even with good intentions we can, and often do, make mistakes. They must remember this when they encounter what may feel like disrespect or when they inadvertently act in an inappropriate manner. Practice asking questions that will help them acquire the knowledge they may need when faced with people whose religious practices are different.

Those of us who maintain a religious faith draw from it comfort, courage, and compassion for our fellow human beings. By helping your children experience this from your own faith, you will be helping them avoid building religious biases.

Some Religions of the World

Baha'i
Baptist
Buddhist
Catholic
Church of Christ
Episcopal
Hindu
Jehovah's Witness
Jewish
Lutheran
Methodist
Mormon
Moslem
Nazarene
Presbyterian
Quaker
Unitarian

Culture and
Ethnicity

"The name 'America' was given to this continent by a German mapmaker, Martin Waldseemuller, to honor an Italian explorer, Amerigo Vespucci. The three ships which discovered America sailed under a Spanish flag, were commanded by an Italian sea captain, and included in their crew an Englishman, an Irishman, a Jew, and a Negro."

— John F. Kennedy

Our cultural differences offer us perhaps the greatest sources for the celebration of diversity. Culture can be defined as the pattern of daily life learned by a group of people, including religion, language, governing practices, art, customs, holiday celebrations, food, dating rituals, and clothes. Kids can see and hear the contributions various cultures have made to our society — from jazz to salsa, tacos to sushi, place-names to fashions, painting to literature. Our language itself reflects our multicultural world: "squash," "succotash," and "barbecue" are Native American words; "banjo," "jambalaya," and "yam" come from Africa; "fiesta," "patio," and "cafeteria" are Spanish.

When most children ask the inevitable question, "Where did I come from?" they are not usually seeking an answer about their cultural identity. By the age of five, they begin to understand that they have descended from somewhere. They know they are identified with a nationality, ethnicity, or cultural background, or a combination of these. As we mentioned earlier, be careful to listen to what your child is truly asking when such questions arise. A popular joke is a keen reminder of this:

A father, who when faced with the question, "Where did I come from?" stops what he's doing, sits his son on his lap, and launches into the lengthy and very detailed sex education speech he has been practicing for months. He drags out the pictures he has prepared and even the book he has purchased for his son to get more information on his own.

Exhausted, he asks his son, "So . . . what do you think? Does everything I've said make sense to you?"

"Well . . ." his son replies, "that's interesting, I thought I came from New York."

We are a nation of people who came from other parts of the world but have not become the melting pot envisioned by many of our ancestors. Instead, today society can be viewed as:

◆ A patchwork quilt — Each square in the quilt is comprised of its own unique design, and these squares are stitched together by the common thread called America; or

◆ A mosaic — Each of us is a tile of a different shape, style, and color. Yet collectively we create a beautiful piece of art; or

◆ A tossed salad — We are all vegetables in the bowl. The cucumber remains a cucumber when the tomato moves in. The lettuce is still lettuce when the onions hit the bowl. Yet each vegetable's flavor is enhanced by being placed next to a different vegetable. And once a common dressing is applied, the individual vegetables form a salad.

Our forefathers' initial description of this nation, *e pluribus unum* — from many, one — held no requirement that the many give up what makes them unique in order to become part of the one. Our nation's strength is in diversity.

The first step to building children's appreciation of the contributions of all cultures is to TELL them where the things they enjoy come from. A teenager who can't get enough hip-hop music might be interested to know it is a rebirth of the African oral and drum tradition. The toddler who wants to eat nothing but McDonald's fries can learn she's actually eating a French food. The preteen who spends hours painting her nails can discover she is practicing an ancient Asian art of body decoration.

Helping kids understand how truly multicultural our society is, as they taste, touch, smell, hear, and see the world around them, can have two significant effects. First, it will negate the possibility that they will grow to believe that one type of person created the American experience and, as such, has more right to enjoy and benefit from it. Second, knowing that we draw on a wide range of cultures on a daily basis can go a long way toward keeping our children from thinking that their particular cultural niche is all-encompassing and that other customs are strange.

Remember the "four questions exercise" we suggested during our discussion of racial differences, and now consider what cultural identifiers you used when describing yourself. Think about the traditions in your own culture that have been important to you and what you want to teach your children. If you were asked to define your own cultural identity, what would you say? In what ways did you become aware of it, learn about it? What traditions have you come to treasure? Do you continue to practice them? What values from your culture do you not agree with or practice? Finally, what cultural values do you want to pass on to your children?

Ask yourself and whoever is sharing in the responsibility of raising your children these questions. Create a list of ways in which you can help your children learn and appreciate their rich cultural heritage. Be sure that your plans allow for your children to understand how their unique heritage enhances their identity as Americans rather than detracts from it.

Share your good memories with your kids. Let them experience the closeness of family and community. Bring them to gatherings and festive occasions filled with music, food, and other traditions special to you. They will feel a connection to their cultural heritage, a deep sense of belonging. And be sure that they receive explanations for what they are experiencing so that they will not perceive them as just eating and dancing experiences.

Learning to value their own culture and ethnic traditions helps kids understand that others also have their own sets of values. Just as your children must know who they are, they need to be encouraged to expand their knowledge by learning about those around them. Make conscious efforts to step outside your cultural box by exposing your children to other people's rich traditions. Research your community for museums, exhibits, or programs of other cultures. Ask friends and other caregivers to share their stories and traditions. Create a family project in which your older children actually do a bit of research on a particular culture, culminating in an evening of foods and games from that culture. Select various styles of music to listen and dance to and discuss the roots of them with your children.

> **Learning to value their own culture and ethnic traditions helps kids understand that others also have their own sets of values.**

Most important, continuously reinforce the idea that respect for people whose customs and beliefs are different from theirs is nonnegotiable. Even before they know what cultural differences mean, kids can feel respect for them.

Reacting to Differences

Often, though, even the most respectful kids react to cultural and ethnic differences with laughter and avoidance. In children, these initial reactions are usually masking curiosity, fear, or lack of comfort with the unfamiliar rather than expressing bias. The example of Lourdes's mother in Chapter 1 is a good one to follow if your child is getting a reaction to your language, food, dress, or other customs. Showing your child how to share her culture may prevent negative attitudes from developing.

Additionally, as we discussed in the section about religion, it is important that your children know how to ask questions when they witness something they don't understand. Help them see that we each have filters through which we view the world. These filters come from a lifetime of experiences. When we see something new, we often interpret it incorrectly based on previous, unrelated information. For example, when someone slightly bows rather than shakes your hand, you may assume he is being "standoffish" if you don't know that in his culture bowing is a sign of respect. Or when a woman holds out her hand for a handshake by a man and it is not taken, she may feel rejected if she does not know that his cultural practices prevent him from touching a woman. Or when your child offers a bite of his candy to another child who reacts by telling him that he can't eat that food, your child may feel hurt if he does not understand the other child's cultural dietary restrictions. Practice asking questions with your younger children so that they will feel comfortable finding the information they'll need to grow up as respectful members of a multi-cultural society.

If your child is reacting poorly — teasing, laughing, avoiding — to someone from another culture simply because he or she is "different," you'll want to help him reach out for understanding before the culture gap becomes the basis for exclusion and bias. But first make sure your child understands that this behavior is not acceptable to you. Then help him determine how he is feeling and examine his own behavior. Point out what your child and the victim of his prejudice have in common. Next, discuss the differences. Remind your child how important his culture is to him as a way of understanding how the other person must feel about his or her own culture. Consider activities that might expose your child to this particular culture in ways that will engage him.

"Having grown up in a small and quiet family, I was somewhat unprepared for my first experience with my best friend's large Italian family. The opera music was blaring — the pasta just kept coming — and they used Italian words and expressions that I had never heard before, much less understood. But — the joy was contagious. I soon found myself singing along, and the next day I bought an Italian dictionary. Next time, I'll be ready!"

Many cultures share similar stories and customs as ways of teaching their children. Let your children know about these similarities as you discover them. There is a story from both Jewish and African culture that gives a wonderful description of heaven and hell that is also a lesson in how we treat one another. This is the Jewish version:

The Hasidic Jews describe heaven and hell as the same basic scene. Hell consists of a very, very, very long table surrounded by many, many chairs. In each chair sits a person who is very, very hungry, almost starving. In the middle of the table sits a pot of the most delicious, nutritious, wonderful-smelling soup. And the people are salivating from the aroma — anticipating the taste of it. Each person is given a very long-handled spoon. They use their spoons to reach into the pot, turn the spoons around to eat, but the handles are so long that they hit their faces and the soup spills. Thus, hell is one continuous seeking for fulfillment without ever getting it met.

In heaven, the same scene exists. There is a very, very, very long table surrounded by many, many chairs. In each chair sits a person who is very, very hungry, almost starving. In the middle of the table sits a pot of the most delicious, nutritious, wonderful-smelling soup. And the people are salivating from the aroma — anticipating the taste of it. Each person is given a very long-handled spoon. Except that in heaven, instead of dipping into the pots and turning their spoons around, hitting their faces, and spilling the soup, they dip into the pot and then reach across the table and feed one another.

We must help our children to learn how to dip into their own pots, reach across cultures, and feed one another.

Greetings from Around the World

India: The <u>namaste</u> — Place your hands in a praying position at the chest and bow slightly.

Israel: Shake hands or embrace, depending on how well you know the person, while saying <u>Shalom</u>.

Japan: Bow from the waist to a fifteen-degree angle. This is an informal bow used for all ranks and occasions.

Latin America: Hug (this is called an <u>abrazo</u>) and give a few hearty claps on the back.

Malays of Malaysia: Stretch out your hands and touch fingertips with the other person. Then bring your hands to your heart, signifying, "I greet you from my heart." Men may only use this gesture with other men and women may only use it with other women.

Middle East: The <u>salaam</u> — Sweep your right hand upward, first touching your heart, then your forehead, and finally up and outward. Accompany this gesture by the phrase "<u>Salaam alaykum</u>," which means "Peace be with you."

Polynesia: Embrace and rub each other's backs. (This is a gesture performed only by men.)

Russia: Shake hands firmly. Follow with a bear hug.

Southern Europe, Central and South America: Shake hands warmly and linger a bit longer than the traditional American handshake. Follow by touching the other person's forearm, elbow, or lapel.

United States: Shake hands firmly and make direct eye contact.

Differences of Ability

Historically, people with physical and mental disabilities have been feared, hidden, or ignored entirely. Noticing differences in ability can make us uncomfortable. As young as two years of age, children voice their curiosity and sometimes fear of physical and mental differences in ability. They want to sit in wheelchairs, try on leg braces, and know why Mary has a "little radio" in her ear. If they are allowed to ask questions and examine the devices people use to help themselves, kids can learn not to be wary. They can appreciate one another's individual abilities and talents.

We can help kids understand that physical and mental abilities are only one aspect of a person. And we can remind them that all people have many abilities, if we will only focus on what they CAN do.

Kids, especially when they're little, often relate very easily without bias to people with disabilities. Think about it: Young children have yet to grow into their *own* full abilities and, in a sense, are limited in ability themselves. Lack of large motor skills makes learning to ride a tricycle the kind of challenge that helps a child easily relate to learning to power a wheelchair. Coached past their fears, most children will let their curiosity lead them to unbiased respect for people who have a disability and to form genuine relationships with these individuals.

We must help our children understand that all of us have a variety of abilities and inabilities. We excel at some things and find other things difficult or

impossible. Take the time to explain physical disabilities to your children. Help them understand
that for some people, differences in their bodies may
make it more difficult or impossible to do some
things others take for granted. This does not make
them more or less of a person.

One way to make this point is to discuss our
abilities with our children, comparing and contrast-
ing their own with ours. Ask yourself, "What are my
own greatest strengths? What are my greatest weak-
nesses?" Every one of us can probably readily name
the qualities we like best and least in ourselves.
Maybe you're awkward on the skating rink, but you
can dance until dawn without one false step. You
know every word of your favorite songs, even
though you can't carry a tune. You're not much
good at writing, but you can paint beautiful land-
scapes. You've always been hopeless at math, but
you can fix anything from broken toilets to toasters.
Think about your own abilities and how you developed them:

◆   What do you do best?

◆   How did you discover your abilities?

◆ How do you challenge your abilities as an adult?

◆ How do you relate to people whose abilities are different from yours?

◆ How do you identify and encourage your children's abilities?

Have your children do this, too. Ask them what they think they do best, what they have difficulty with. Discuss a time when they had to work harder than anyone else to accomplish something. Point out a special talent that a sibling or friend might have and talk about how it feels to admire it or even at times to be jealous of it. Help your child see that within each of us lie special talents. Our differences in abilities expand our experiences and bring us closer together.

"Four-year-old Tim, who has Down's syndrome, is pulling the wagon around the playground. It's one of his favorite activities. His classmate Elena joins him and gets into the wagon. She announces to the nearby teacher: 'He's a messy painter, but he's a good wagon puller.'"

**PEOPLE WITH SPECIAL NEEDS
MAY ALSO HAVE VERY SPECIAL GIFTS:**

- **Alexander the Great had epilepsy.**

- **Ludwig van Beethoven was deaf.**

- **Sarah Bernhardt, the actress, had a leg amputated.**

- **Winston Churchill stuttered.**

- **Thomas Edison was hearing impaired and learning disabled.**

- **Vincent van Gogh was emotionally disturbed.**

- **Helen Keller was blind and deaf.**

Conclusion

People are different. Explaining these differences in a way that promotes respect and prevents bias is a challenge. Rising to the occasion begins with each of us examining our own experiences and feelings. In the next chapter, as we explore how differences we perceive lead to hate, ask yourself:

◆ To what extent am I honest with my children, especially about my own hurt and anger?

◆ What messages do I send my children to help them cope with injustice and hate?

◆ What messages did I receive from my parents about these subjects and what role do those messages play in my life today?

"If there is anything that we wish to change in the child, we should first examine it and see whether it is not something that could be better changed in ourselves."

— Carl Gustav Jung

CHAPTER 3

Why Do People Hate?

"She came home in tears. It took almost a half hour before she could speak in a way that I could understand because she was crying so hard. First, all I heard was 'They wouldn't play with me,' and I thought that she and her two best friends had had yet another fight — the kind that happens frequently when three little girls play together each day. But the look on her face and the level of her anxiety let me know it was more. 'One of them said that her mommy said I was a _____ and that we were dirty and no good,' she finally said. I was shocked. What could I say?"

"We had had a number of conversations about the Civil Rights Movement and even about what his grandparents had experienced in the late fifties. But nothing prepared me for my son's sophomore year. It started out great. He made the varsity basketball team and even started in the second game. He had a group of friends and seemed truly comfortable and happy. One week I noticed he was a bit quieter than usual. By the weekend, his silence was deafening. I was surprised to find him home on Saturday evening instead of out with his group of guys. I asked him where everyone was and he told me Lisa M. was having a party. She had initially invited him but on Monday told him she had to uninvite him. She liked him and was really sorry, but her parents thought it was wrong to have him there. He quoted her final statement: 'After all, people should only date their own kind and a party might lead to dating.' And then he added, 'I thought we were friends, Dad. What did I do?'"

When our children hurt, we hurt. In the pits of our stomachs we begin to feel their pain, simultaneously marrying it to the pain we may have felt in similar situations ourselves. Perhaps you remember in your young life turning to an adult when someone did something to hurt you and asking "Why?" It's a hard question, and our own parents and caregivers may not have known how to answer it.

When we are faced with this same question from our own children, we struggle to find a reasonable explanation for unreasonable behavior. Coupled with the anger we may feel toward those who have hurt our children, we seek to find an answer that might somehow break a cycle that is far older than ourselves. This situation, like countless others that we experience in our role in the day-to-day development of a child, reminds us yet again that no one has all the answers every time.

However, it is important to talk with our children about hate *before* they encounter a specific situation, to prepare them with options for responding to what happens "out there," and prevent them from becoming the people making it happen. Talking proactively also helps you discuss reasons and responses at a time when your own emotions are in check, not when you are struggling between gritted teeth or when your child's feelings are so hurt that no answer will suffice.

What Is Hate and Why Do People Feel It?

For the purposes of this book, let's talk about hate as a strong negative response to differences. If we think about a wide range of responses to differences along a continuum, respect and understanding would be at one end and hate would be at the other. Respect includes acknowledging all people's differences. Hate includes disapproving of other people who are seen as "different" and assuming the right to feel and act in hateful ways toward people we see as "different."

Somewhere between these two poles is the concept of tolerance, recognizing that others have the

> **The genesis of hate is fear and ignorance.**

right to be who they are, but tolerance falls short of respect and understanding. The genesis of hate is fear and ignorance. Hate can also be a response to having been hated, the proverbial vicious circle.

Hating Out of Ignorance and Untrue Information

"On Labor Day my husband, my son, and I went with my mom, my dad, my two sisters, and their families to Bluewater Lake for a picnic. We are Mexicans, and one of my sisters is married to Harry, who is African-American. They have two sons. Bluewater Lake is a very small lake with a small park area. There were four other families there that day, one Pakistani family, another Mexican family, one mixed family like us, Hispanics and African-Americans, and one white family. It was such a beautiful day and we were all having a good time. My husband, my sisters, and our kids were in the water by the beach when the two kids from the white family joined us in the water. We were playing with them when their father from far away yelled at them, 'Kids, kids, remember what I told you; do not go near those minorities!'

"I just could not believe my ears. Against my husband's will I got out of the water and approached the man. As I got closer, I noticed that his body was covered with tattoos. I went to him and in a very calm voice told him, 'You know, sir, I do not think it is such a good idea to teach hatred toward other people to your kids.'

"He then responded, 'That's how I grew up. That's what my parents always told me.'

"I asked him, 'Do you think it is a good idea to pass on your parents' mistakes to your kids? Would you like your kids to have all that hatred in their hearts like you do? I know that in five minutes I am not going to change the way you think, but I can assure you that you are doing more harm than good to your kids by teaching them hatred. What you should teach them is to be smart enough to differentiate between good and bad. We may be Hispanic, but we are not bad people. Would you like to see your son on TV one day showing how many kids he has shot, just like the one who shot all those Jewish kids a few days ago? You can be sure that this guy grew up in a house with as much hatred as the one your kids are growing up in.'

"His wife approached me and said, 'Why don't you just worry about your own kid?'

"I was holding my six-month-old son. I told her, 'That's exactly why I decided to come and say those words to your husband, because I worry about my son's safety. Now more than ever I worry about hate in the world. Perhaps if I did not worry about my son, I would have just felt sorry for your husband and your family. But because of my son I believe I should speak up and try to make a little difference in this world as far as hate is concerned.'

"She just looked at me and said, 'Well, that's how he grew up.'

"I then responded, 'For your kids' sake,

you should ask him to seek help,' and I walked away.

"As I was walking away the man said, 'This world would still be better if you guys were not here.'

"At that point I felt unsafe and decided to call the police. The police officer arrived and we all went to talk to the man. My husband told him, 'You know what? Maybe you cannot control what is in your heart. All that hatred was planted in you, but you sure can control your mouth.'

"'Look,' he said, pointing to a KKK tattoo he had on his arm. 'I am a member of the KKK and that's why I have to say what I have to say.'

"My husband told him, 'I am sure you have not read enough about that group, otherwise you would not be so proud to say you are a member. Good luck, because you need it.' And we walked away.

"The police officer then came to us and told us that the man said he was now going to behave and not say anything else, but I told the police officer that I did not feel safe with him around. We had just started our fire to cook lunch and we were not prepared to leave because of him. I told the officer that we wanted the man removed from the park. The police officer then went to tell him what we had said and he agreed to leave after he finished eating his hot dogs.

"It was such a good feeling to have said what I said to him. Like I told him, I know that I am not going to change his mind, but perhaps next time he will not be so willing to expose his hatred to the world. And who knows? Maybe he will also think a little of what I told him.

"We had lunch at the park and despite this incident, we had a good time!"

"Kids, Kids, Remember What I Told You. . . ."

The man at Bluewater Lake who calls his children out of the water and away from "those minorities" gives the narrator this reason for his words: "That's what my parents always told me."

Parents' attitudes and behaviors shape their children's. Parents are usually the first examples children have to follow, and children often accept their parents' beliefs without question. So much of prejudice is simply passed along, unchallenged, from parents to children, sometimes for generations. Children don't always have the opportunities to learn that biased attitudes are based on not knowing, on making prejudgments about people because those people are seen as "different." This is hate based on ignorance, on not knowing.

But sometimes hate is based on thinking or assuming something that is simply untrue. In the first scenario in this chapter, the information the two little girls were given — that the third child was "dirty and no good" — is not true but powerful. If you have learned either overtly or subtly to interact with people based on certain cultural group differences, you will likely do so almost without feeling that you are being prejudiced. Many who hate out of ignorance do not know any other way. Most people have not examined their attitudes in light of their effect on others; they are genuinely ignorant. "I don't have anything against those people; I just feel more comfortable sticking with my own kind" is often the core of such thinking.

Such prejudices are often so habitual that they are almost unconscious. When they are allowed to

take root in us when we're young, they are often difficult to uproot, as the narrator of the Bluewater
Lake story acknowledges when she tells the man, "I
know that in five minutes I am not going to change
the way you think." The understanding that we
need to make informed, fair judgments about other
people remains out of reach because of the prejudice. We avoid certain groups of people because of
the untrue information we have about them —
"those people are like that." We repeat labels and
stereotypes because "that's what my parents said."
And some of these prejudices have become so much
a part of the fabric of our society, we hardly think of
them as prejudices — they are simply the way
things are, the norm.

Hating Out of Fear of the Unfamiliar

In addition to ignorance and having untrue infor-
mation, hate can result from sheer unfamiliarity.
We prefer our own ways, the "taste of home."
When someone looks or acts or thinks differently

than we do, we can easily feel afraid. The unfamiliar — from foods we're not used to to languages we don't understand — can be intimidating. When we deal with our fears of the unfamiliar by forming negative attitudes, by avoidance, or by unkind actions, we are exercising hate.

Sometimes our fear of people we see as different from ourselves is expressed so subtly it is unspoken. If we hesitate when our child asks to visit the home of a classmate of a different race or religion, we are still communicating our own discomfort with the idea. Whether we mean to or not, we have become the unwitting agent of negative messages about another person, group, or neighborhood. The parents in the Lisa M. scenario were afraid of the unfamiliar — the potential for dating across racial lines. Fear and discomfort with others who are different from ourselves are often masked by "should" rules whose underpinnings are basically separatist, like the one Lisa M. spouted: "People should only date their own kind."

When we find ourselves believing apparently benign "shoulds," we are likely harboring unconscious hate. We "should" be able to have our own neighborhood in which to exercise our faith and culture without others moving in; we don't move into their

> **Live and let live often masquerades as respect, but it is a subtle form of hate.**

communities. We "should" be able to have our own schools that express our culture without others getting to enroll here; "they" have their own schools. "Live and let live" often masquerades as respect, but it is a subtle form of hate.

"I Am a Member of ____. That's Why I Have to Say What I Have to Say. . . ."

Paradoxically, the other side of fear and the discomfort with the unfamiliar that produces hate is the desire to belong. We want to be part of the group with which we *are* familiar so we know we are accepted.

The man in the Bluewater Lake story points to his KKK tattoo as another "reason" for his attitudes. Some groups make hatred of others a condition of membership. The security we feel with those who look and think like us produces and reinforces prejudice against those who don't look and think the same way. Our group identity becomes more impor-

tant than our individual differences and is strength-
ened by excluding, even targeting, others.

Organized hatred often disguises itself as something else. In its most extreme forms, it finds a
"righteous" rationale for its acts of prejudice, claim-
ing its agenda is somehow contributing to the overall good of humanity. Such hatred may masquerade
as racial purity or religious zeal or the need for security or just sheer self-preservation.

In its less severe forms, hate born out of fear gets
passed off as "just being one of the gang," in kidding around, or justified with words like, "Oh, come
on, you know I don't really mean it." These "innocent" prejudices often arise out of a group mentality,
in-jokes intended to exclude others, or attitudes of
superiority toward outsiders. Intentionally hurtful or
not, these actions can cause severe emotional pain.

**"There was really nothing wrong at all with
this girl. As I think about it, she was no different from me and my friends. But I was so
ignorant in junior high, I guess I blocked out
all common sense in order to fit in with the
cool crowd. And please don't take this the
wrong way — this group that I hung out with
are still some of my closest friends. They**

never said anything like, 'Oh, today we're going to be mean again.' I think that we felt
that if we were all doing it, it must be right. I
know that as we persisted in humiliating this
girl, we all had thoughts like, 'This is wrong,'
and 'Why are we doing this?'

"I was so two-faced! I would smile at her
whenever I wasn't with my friends, and
every time she managed to send her beautiful smile right back. I even went for a day
with her to her summer cottage, and I spent
a lot of weekends over at her house, learning
more and more about the wonderful person
my friends and I made fun of every day in
school. I know that she was nice to me and
had never said anything nasty about me, but
at the time it felt to me like I had no choice; I
could be her friend or be with my other
friends, not both. Even though at times I felt
sorry for her and asked myself what was
making me treat her like this, I still made no
attempt to stop the group's foolish activities
against her.

"The point I am trying to make is we
sometimes try so hard to fit into a group that
we don't realize the consequences. . . . Did I

mention that because of me this girl went to another school for her freshman year? . . . In November of 1997 she died in a car accident, and I will never be able to apologize to her. . . . I wish I could have just stood up for her and told my friends what a great person she was instead of spreading rumors. . . .

"I hope that anyone who hears this story will learn to be able to stand up for someone whom you would normally laugh at. I hope that you can go up to someone sitting alone in the cafeteria and ask him or her to join you. But most of all, I hope that you can correct all of your wrongs before it is too late. Because, believe me, it is much easier to forgive yourself after apologizing to someone's face than it is to forgive yourself after apologizing through prayer."

The fear of not belonging is strong in most children. In adolescence, as children begin the process of breaking away from their families, they search for other avenues of belonging. Some children exclude or make fun of other people because they believe it is the popular thing to do. Some begin to use unkind names for different groups of people in an attempt to make them feel more accepted by their peers.

It took a terrible loss for the girl who rejected her friend to realize the consequences of her behavior. Now she tries to keep other teens from repeating her mistakes by telling her story publicly. If you find out that your own child is one who hates, there are early steps you can take to help her value, respect, and have sensitivity for other people's feelings more than for peer acceptance.

Haters derive pleasure from belittling others to make themselves feel better. Children who have poor self-images are more vulnerable to the desire to belong to "their own group" and thereby develop prejudices against perceived "others." They may try to bolster their own flagging self-worth by finding a group of people to put down. An insecure child might think, "I may not be very good, but I am better than those people." For some, putting down others may serve as a psychological function, allowing them to feel more important and powerful than those they put down.

"I Believe I Should Speak Up. . . ."

The Bluewater Lake story and the others told here show us several truths about the hatred that comes from ignorance and fear:

◆ Parents can teach children to hate; they can also teach them not to hate. Our children absorb our attitudes, even those we don't know we have.

◆ Lack of information about people whom we see as different from ourselves sets the stage for hatred.

◆ Fear of being "not good enough," or not belonging, or not being "popular" can draw children to exercise hateful words and actions.

◆ Parents and children can stand up to hatred.

By teaching self-respect and empathy and by offering information and exposure to diversity, we can help our children "to be smart enough to differentiate between good and bad," not ignorant and fearful enough to hate.

Hating Out of
Hurt and Anger

**"When I was in junior high school, the kids
in my class made fun of me because I was
Bengali. They would say, 'Why are you here?
Why don't you fly away on your magic car-
pet; you're not wanted here.' This tore me up
inside. I wanted to beat the crap out of
them."**

When hate and derision have been directed at us
or at our children, it's a natural impulse to feel
hurt and anger. Civil rights activist Medgar
Evers was murdered by a white man in Jackson,
Mississippi, as he was getting out of his car at home
on the night of June 12, 1963. Evers's widow, Myrlie,
has talked about her feelings that night:

**"After they took Medgar's lifeless body away,
and the police came, and some neighbors
came who were white, and I walked outside
of our door and saw the blood that had been
wasted from his body and saw them standing
there in uniforms, all I could see was the**

**color of their skins. And I hated everyone
who was white . . . I literally wanted to get a
machine gun and just mow people down, just
take lives."**

Myrlie Evers admits that she found a kind of sustenance in the strength of her hatred:

**"I'm not sure I would have existed without
that . . . after Medgar's death, because it
gave me a fire and a fuel to keep going. Perhaps that sounds very negative, but that's a
part of what hatred does. Perhaps we can
say in a sense it was very positive for me. If I
had not had that strong hatred, I think I
would have collapsed totally."**

And yet she also eventually realized that the negative effects of her hatred began to outweigh the positive:

**"Hatred can become intensified to a point
where it's almost an illness. It was something
I had to get out of my system. The sound of
'Dixie' being played on the radio . . . the
voice of elected officials, particularly the**

governor, made this heat from the pit of my stomach rise through my chest and my throat and spew out . . . seeing the Confederate flag waving . . . that was hatred, and it was destroying me. It wasn't the way to continue my life. . . ."

For many members of groups who have been systematically oppressed or have been traditionally the objects of routine societal bias, this hatred may feel as natural as breathing. It can be expressed as cynicism, wariness, coldness, or hardness toward all those of the "oppressor" group. The continuing realities of institutional and individual bias make such self-protective attitudes understandable. There are times when it is not humanly possible to counter hate or respond in any way but to feel the hurt, absorb the hate, and feel anger and hate toward the haters.

Accepting "righteous indignation" in ourselves and encouraging our children to examine and accept this in themselves when they are the objects of intense, routine, or systematically condoned bias is healthy. Making that our ONLY response to bias is not. Neither is holding responsible those who had no role in, did not condone, and do not accept advantages resulting from the biased acts.

Hate is a natural initial response to egregious deeds of hate, but it is never an acceptable long-term response to differences in individuals. The Holocaust, the Transatlantic Passage, "ethnic cleansings" in eastern Europe, are all horrible acts of hate. Our feelings of hurt and our anger are justified. But to pick out characteristics of those who perpetrated such crimes and hate others who happen to have those characteristics is like refusing to ever eat again if you have a meal that makes you sick. Anger and even hate can produce positive efforts toward righting injustice, but hatred toward those who hurt you may overpower every other reaction and become all-consuming and self-destructive.

For many who have felt the pain and anger of having been hated, refusing to hate is easier said than done. But as Myrlie Evers learned, there are ways of coping with hate other than letting it take firm root in ourselves. Her own children helped her find another way to go on:

". . . perhaps the most important part of the change came about when my three children looked at me in complete dismay and they would say to me, 'Momma, Daddy said we shouldn't hate.' And I realized that I was giv-

ing mixed messages to them. And I realized that was something that I could not do to my children. Nor could I do it to myself. Nor could I do it to Medgar's memory."

Letting go of hatred and anger when they are no longer appropriate is a huge challenge. It starts with the conscious decision to let go of responses that are no longer useful and "let in" others whom you label as part of the hurting group. Letting relationships develop, seeing people as individuals rather than as members of the offending group is an important first step.

Understanding that there are levels and degrees of bias and that we have a choice of responses is key to reframing attitudes that are destructive and limiting.

"My parents came to this country in the late 1930s from Germany. They were among the lucky ones who got out, unlike many members of their families who died in concentration camps. I was born in the United States. When I was growing up, my parents always wanted to look ahead; they didn't like to talk about the old country very much. They al-

ways spoke German at home, and I remember wishing they sounded like the other kids' parents. I wished my father knew how to throw a baseball. My parents didn't say much about Germans, even Nazis, but I knew they had a lot of feelings about them; it was something we just didn't talk about.

"When I was a junior in high school, I applied for a summer student exchange program in Germany. My parents didn't say anything about that, either. They didn't seem happy about my going, but they didn't seem to mind it, either. The night before I left to go away I heard my mother scream in the night, and when I went into my parents' room to see what had happened, my mother was crying. She told me she had been dreaming of ovens. She knew it didn't make sense, but she said she was scared to let me go to Germany."

Even when we don't express our hurt out loud it can invade our consciousness in dreams. In this house the parents rarely spoke about the pain of exile. It took the thought of their son's trip to Germany to release their suppressed anguish.

Role Models for Overcoming Hatred

Turning hurt and anger away from hatred and toward understanding is one of the hardest lessons of being human. Our greatest teachers may be those who, like Myrlie Evers, suffered almost impossible pain and loss and then found the strength to move to acceptance of our common humanity.

Nelson Mandela spent twenty-seven years as a political prisoner in South Africa for his opposition to the system of apartheid. "I could have spent a long time in prison and wasted away the most productive years of my life," he says.

"Those conditions would make any man very bitter and his heart to be full of hate. There was a lot of cruelty . . . [but] you must also understand the wardens who worked with us . . . are themselves human beings with problems, who are also exploited, the victims of the system. And one of our objectives was to ensure that we improved the relations be-

**tween ourselves and these wardens, help
them in their own problems. In that way, you
forget about anything that is negative like
hate. You are dealing with human beings
and you want to live in peace with these
people. You want them also to go and spread
the message to their own people. . . ."**

Maired Maguire, who lost four members of her
family as a result of the conflict in Northern Ireland,
has devoted her life to the peaceful resolution of differences that can otherwise lead to violence and
death:

**"On the tenth of August 1976, my young sis-
ter took her three children out for a walk. A
short time later, all three children were
killed. . . . My sister recovered, thank God,
and she had two more little children. But in
January 1980, on a cold winter day, she took
her own life. Because she couldn't go on."**

When asked what she would say if she were able
to meet the man who had shot the children,
Maguire answers:

"The day my sister's three children were buried, I went to see Mrs. Lannon, who was the mother of the young IRA man, Danny Lannon, who had driven the car. Danny Lannon was shot through the head by the Security Forces. And Mrs. Lannon was heartbroken because she had lost a son. Her son was the product of a society with nothing to hope for, no dignity. And somehow driving a car and opening fire on soldiers was an expression of that anger.

"I don't want to see any more Danny Lannons having to be shot through the head by soldiers in my own street, or any more Mrs. Lannons having to suffer that. So I would say to any young man who passionately, passionately wants to change the world: 'Practice nonviolence. Use the techniques of nonviolence to change your world.'"

President of the Czech Republic, poet, and playwright, Václav Havel, who was imprisoned many times for his criticism of the communist regime in Czechoslovakia, remembers hatred directed at him during that time:

"A prison warden hated me almost patholog-
ically. . . . Once he told me he would love to
shoot me if he could." But when asked, "Did
you feel any desire to repay hate with hate?"
Havel answered, "I'm not capable of really
hating. . . . Sometimes there are people who
bother me, who drive me crazy. . . . But I don't
remember [feeling] out-and-out hatred. My
entire life, I have never experienced that.
And I think it has helped me very much.
Because hatred, among other things, doesn't
allow you to see the world clearly and
objectively."

In the testimony of all these survivors, the way
to overcome hatred is to see the haters as they have
been unable to see those whom they have hated
and hurt: to see them as human beings rather than
as "strangers."

"Momma, Daddy Said We Shouldn't Hate. . . ."

Parents can draw several lessons from these stories
of dealing with the hurt and anger of being hated:

◆ They can teach their children to acknowledge pain and anger when they are objects of hate and still teach their children not to hate.

◆ Our children need to hear stories of overcoming oppression and surviving with triumphant attitudes. We need to tell children our personal stories of triumph and defeat.

◆ All people need to learn to distinguish individuals who do specific hateful acts from people who are similar to those doing the acts.

◆ Fear that bad situations will never change can lead children to feel hopeless, which can lead them to use hateful words and do hurtful deeds.

◆ Parents need to take appropriate and rational action to handle biased acts.

◆ Parents need to provide models of success so children can see that some people have successfully stood up to hatred.

◆ By teaching self-respect and self-empowerment, parents can help children combat hate without resorting to hate.

Conclusion

All forms of hatred destroy human possibilities. From unspoken, sometimes unconscious, biases to adolescent "in-group" behavior to organized and institutionalized oppression, hatred poisons relationships, divides communities and countries, deprives people of their rights, causes psychological and emotional pain, and can lead to violence, war, and death.

As Elie Wiesel, Holocaust survivor and Nobel Peace Prize winner has testified, "Even hate of hate is dangerous."

Ignorance and fear, hurt and anger do pervasive damage to all people's lives. Parents can prevent much of the damage by providing home environments that educate and make their children comfortable with differences, and by addressing the feelings and attitudes that lead to hatred.

In Chapter 4, we will show you how to develop the skills you need to accomplish this.

What Can We Do About Hate?

"I had been saving my money from my after-school job for almost three months to buy the basketball shorts I wanted. They were pretty pricey, but I wanted them, and anyway, it was my money. I finally had enough to buy the shorts and I worried all day that when I went to the store they would be sold out of the ones I wanted. But they were there, and I bought them, and I was practically singing out loud as I walked out the door! Until I got to the exit. I was stopped there by two huge security guards and a police officer who had been called by the store, and they grabbed me and they grabbed my bag with the shorts out of my hands and accused me of stealing the shorts. I was so surprised I wasn't even scared at the time. I could barely talk, but I finally managed to say, 'I just bought these shorts.' Then one of the store security guards turned the bag upside down and my new shorts fell on the floor. Seeing them on the dirty floor made me want to cry but, of course, I didn't. 'So, where's the receipt, if you just bought these shorts?' the guard said. I turned that bag upside down and inside out looking for the receipt, but it wasn't in there. 'I don't know,' I said, and I looked down at the ground because I didn't want them to see my face. 'I think we'd better keep these shorts right here,' the guard said, 'because proof of purchase is a requirement for exiting this store.' I knew that wasn't true because no one else was being stopped at the exit, but I didn't have any choice and I left the store without my shorts. To tell you the truth, I really didn't even want them anymore. When I got home, I told my father what happened, and he got real angry at me and started yelling at me louder than he ever yelled at me before in my whole life. 'Haven't I always told you to keep the receipt? What's

**wrong with you, boy?' He just kept scream-
ing that at me, over and over."**
   — Sixteen-year-old African-American boy

Seeing our children targeted by hate is devas-
tating. It is virtually impossible for us as parents to separate our feelings from our
children's. We are so connected to them emotionally that we can easily get confused about
whose pain is whose. We would gladly suffer any
painful situation for them, if only we could.

When parents see their children hurt, both parents and children suffer. Understanding that and
knowing how to separate our feelings from our children's feelings are the first tasks for parents in helping children deal with hate in their lives. We have to
let them have their own pain. We can't suffer it for
them; nor should we try to take it from them. The
pain is theirs, and they need to learn how to handle
hateful situations.

That does not mean that we can leave them on
their own; we must be there for them. But our actions must not deprive our children of the opportunity to learn important life lessons.

That task becomes complicated when we ourselves have suffered hate and hurt as children and as adults. Consider the father in the situation above. He had learned from an early age to protect himself from possible accusations of theft by holding tight to register receipts. He had wanted to protect his son from the same indignities he suffered and had passed that information on to his son.

"I wanted so much to help my boy! He's my firstborn, with my same name. And he had worked so hard to save money for those shorts. And I saw how sad and hurt he was by the experience in the store. And all I could think of was, well, this wouldn't have happened if he had kept the receipt. The thing I feel worst about is I was so focused on that. I never did even give him a hug, which is probably what he needed. And I blamed him for something that wasn't his fault. Sure, he should have had the receipt. But it was racism that caused that situation, not my son. I directed my anger at my son, but it was the racist situation I was really mad about — and my own sense of powerlessness to protect my son from this kind of hate."

All parents feel pain and anguish when we discover we are powerless to protect our children. We must all learn never to allow our children to become inappropriate targets for our rage. That only compounds our children's pain. The father in the scenario realized in hindsight that despite his own feelings, his son needed comfort. A long bear hug in total silence, because you don't know what to say, can be the best immediate balm for a child who's experienced hate. An embrace with which you let flow your own tears of rage, feelings of helplessness, and pain from past hateful encounters can also start the flow of healing waters for your hurting child.

> **A long bear hug in total silence, because you don't know what to say, can be the best immediate balm for a child who's experienced hate.**

When we vent our feelings on our children, we deprive ourselves and our offspring of the opportunity to address the right target for the situation. While we cannot always protect our children from hate, we are *not* passive players in racist and other hateful dramas. We can respond appropriately and effectively. But it takes practice and, as we stated in the previous chapter, preparation.

Talking to
Your Kids

Some parents are afraid that talking about prejudice will produce it. We often hear, "My kids don't ask me about gender roles or race. Shouldn't I just wait until they *need* to know?" If we do not begin our conversations before there is a problem, we may find ourselves faced with questions that require a great deal of thought, discussion, and explanation during hot, emotional moments. Under these circumstances, even the most practiced of us find it difficult to respond, and our children find it almost impossible to process our responses. Discussing the roots of the disease called hate makes it no more contagious than talking about any other disease. In fact, would you wait to talk with your kids about AIDS or other sexually transmitted diseases until they were infected? Straight, simple talk with kids in preparation for the challenges they might face in life is preventive.

Talking with kids about bias issues is not easy and can be uncomfortable. Think of it as the discomfort of the tiny prick of a needle for an inoculation compared to the immense pain of a dreaded disease. Talking prepares them with responses that will prevent the worst pain and help heal the hurts they may, despite all our efforts, encounter.

Dialogue About Diversity

How we begin and continue our conversations about diversity is dependent upon the maturity of the child with whom you are speaking. The skills we need to talk about effectively with our children change as our children grow. Each child develops differently, and at his or her own pace. The general direction of healthy development — from dependence to independence and from sensory and motor skills to complex emotional, social, and intellectual skills — provides us with the framework in which to operate. Each general stage of development presents children and their parents with unique opportunities for communication, guidance, and learning.

There are a few rules of the road that are consistent regardless of the stage your child is in:

◆ **Treat all of your child's questions with respect and seriousness,** no matter how awkward or embarrassing (or even comical) they may seem to

stakes. Be sure to allow this leeway for your
ell.

und Rules

anklin said it best when she belted out
-C-T. Respect is the key to healthy rela-
and to an environment that teaches
f differences, even differences of opinion. At the heart of having our
children understand and value our
differences is creating a home environment in which children feel
they can express their needs and
views without fear. An atmosphere
of openness not only allows children the freedom to explore different attitudes and activities, it gives
parents the opportunity to know
what their kids are thinking and
how they are feeling. It allows us
to guide them and correct them if
necessary.

ns the basis for the development
. It is never too early to begin to

you. Don't shush, ignore, or dismiss them. If they
make you feel uncomfortable, ask yourself why.
They may be touching on an area that is especially
sensitive for you. Your own discomfort is not a valid
excuse for denying an answer.

◆   **Clarify the question.** It is important that you
understand what is being asked and why. As we saw
in the case of the child who asked, "Where did I
come from?" and got a sex education lecture instead
of a geographic location, we need to make sure we
truly understand what our child is hoping to find
out. It is also important to understand what led to
the question. The teen who asks, "How do you feel
about my dating someone of another faith?" may
be curious about your opinion or may be formulating a response to already having been asked out by
someone of another faith. He or she may be seeking
help in finding an appropriate behavior, not just a
rule or a guideline. A good way to clarify a question
is first to repeat it back and then inquire why you
are being asked or how your child is feeling.

◆   **Answer questions as clearly and honestly as
you can.** Give short, simple answers that your child
can clearly understand and that won't test the limits
of his or her attention span. Don't overexplain. You

can ask if what you've provided is enough and always note that your child should come back for more if needed. Be matter-of-fact. Don't preach. If you do not know the answer, say so and make a plan to find out. Include your child in the plan if possible by saying, "Why don't we go to the library tomorrow and find out?" or "We can call Aunt Esther tonight and ask her — she'll know."

◆ **Correct yourself if you give a "wrong" or incomplete answer.** Don't be afraid of mistakes. Remember, children often make mistakes and are a lot more forgiving of them than most adults. Children also see through attempts to cover up our lack of knowledge. Admitting our mistakes teaches them how to do this when necessary.

◆ **Use appropriate language and definitions.** Our children may not understand the terms we offer in our answers. Be sure that you define terms in a way that is age-appropriate.

◆ **Be alert to signs of upset.** These include withdrawal, lack of interest, acting out, fear of school, or other activities. If you can't draw your child out by asking him or her about it, talk to friends, teachers, and other adults who may be able to help uncover the cause.

◆ **Address any biased** **makes.** You need to prac check your own commen responding to your child

◆ **Teach your chil** Children who yell a ra need to be talked with words are unaccepta Our children must lence doesn't usual based violence sta

◆ **Be sure to** dren who hav biased behav dren or childre They need to gender, acce pearance do

◆ **Allo** Because rience ar may ne Remem that e

make mi
child as

Gro

Aretha Fr
R-E-S-P-E
tionships
acceptance

❝ At the heart of having our children understand and value our differences is creating a home environment in which children feel they can express their needs and views without fear. ❞

Self-respect for
of respect for other

124

126

teach our children the basic rules of respect. As we learned in Chapter 1, their first lesson will come directly from how they are treated by their caregivers. If their individual needs are met with sensitivity and their emerging abilities are encouraged, they will form a strong foundation for the development of respect for others. They will begin to develop their own self-worth.

Respect issues begin early. The advent of preschool usually propels a child into a series of questions about social and cultural rules. "What do I call my teacher?" "Why do we call some people by their first name and only refer to others with a title?" "Why can't I yell in church?" "If I think the hat she is wearing is ugly, what's wrong with telling her so?" "Why do I have to be quiet when an adult is speaking?" And once given a rule to follow, our little free spirits often become the "polite police," pointing out all those who break the rules.

This is a good time to begin a discussion with children about their role in establishing ground rules for respectful behavior and speech:

◆   First, explore the idea of rules, using terms they can understand. It may be helpful to refer to the rules that govern a game they are familiar with.

◆　Talk about how rules are helpful. Ask your children to think of an example of what happens when people do not follow the rules, as well as an example of a time when the rules made it easier to do something. If they have difficulty in understanding what you are asking, provide an example: "Can you imagine if you were trying to play a circle game and no one would stay in the circle?" or "It's a good thing that hide-and-seek requires the seeker to count before he comes looking. How would you hide otherwise?"

◆　Help them understand what the word respect means. See if together you can list five occasions in which they felt respected or five things that make them feel respected. Move the conversation toward identifying ways people act that show respect as well as ways people act that are disrespectful. Discuss how it feels to be respected and disrespected.

◆　Help your children create a list of ways they can show respect for members of your family: "I will not touch my sister's toys without asking." "I will listen when Grandma is speaking." In the case of friends, you might suggest: "I will not make fun of how she does her hair." "I will not ask him to go against something he thinks is right." For people in general, good examples are: "I will not interrupt when someone else is talking." "I will not call people names."

◆ Have your children help you create a list of ways in which they can feel respected. The rules should not be developed only for your children to follow.

My Rights as a Person

- **I have the right to be myself and be treated with respect without regard to any physical characteristics I happen to have.**

- **I have the right to express what I feel in ways that do not hurt others, and no one has the right to ridicule me or hurt my feelings.**

- **I have the right to be understood; I deserve to be listened to.**

- **I have the right to be safe — no one has the right to bully or hurt me physically.**

- **I have the right to grow and learn at my own pace, without being labeled or belittled.**

This is not a one-time discussion. As our children grow and develop, their rules for respect will need to grow and develop. Throughout their lives, it is important to ensure that their own needs for respect are met if we are asking them to adhere to general rules for respecting others.

It is particularly important to revisit the ground rules with teenagers. With the onset of puberty, their need to feel respected is usually great and often hard to meet during this turbulent time.

Respecting Our Differences

How children perceive and value differences is directly related to the way and extent to which they are exposed to those differences. If life is presented as a great adventure to which they have been invited, few children can resist the temptation to join the journey. If the journey's road is presented as treacherous, the familiar path may become their exclusive domain.

Everything children see, hear, taste, and touch in their immediate environment influences their attitudes toward differences. If they learn from the very beginning that people come in all sizes and shapes, colors and cultures, and that they practice different religions, professions, traditions, rites, and rituals, they will accept without fear those who may be different from themselves.

However, human nature often leads us to fear what we are not familiar with. Thus, what children see or experience, as well as what they do *not* see and experience, makes a significant impression upon them.

For example, while we or our parents had to get accustomed to seeing females in certain professions, today our children assume women have always been doctors, lawyers, and executives. Similarly, our children will garner an appreciation for diversity through exposure to it and a matter-of-fact accept-ance and respect.

Our jobs in this process of helping kids respect differences are several:

1. **Teacher:** Start by providing as rich an environ-ment as you can at home to show your children what a wonderful world of difference we live in. Se-lect books that tell stories of different kinds of people or that show diverse groups participating in

everyday activities. Decorate their bedrooms with various photographs, artwork, and crafts. Together try new or different foods; play a variety of music or try out games from around the world. Many libraries offer children's story hours. Bring your children and encourage the librarians to read a diverse set of books. Select a variety of cultural events to attend. Or perhaps study a particular celebration together and then replicate it at home. Your job here is to take responsibility for the lessons you want your child to learn and to actively plan and implement the lessons.

2. **Cheerleader:** Encouragement goes a long way toward accomplishment. Your attitude and support for what your children are being exposed to and how they react to it will have a great impact on the ultimate impression the experience makes. Urge your children on, and applaud their successes. Encourage them to step outside what is comfortable for them by expanding what they do and with whom they usually come in contact. Assist them in identifying activities that will make this happen. Place an obvious value on experiences that allow your children to interact with children from different backgrounds. Cheer on your children in their

attempts to learn more about those who are different from themselves.

3. **Role Model:** Set an example of valuing diversity by your own choices and behaviors. Your friends and colleagues, the people you share fun with and the people you interact with professionally, the businesses you patronize, the events you attend, all send messages to your children about the value you place on diversity. We all know that our children learn more by seeing what we do than by listening to what we say.

Conclusion

ate hurts. Challenging the hate and healing the hurt begin at home. They begin with parents being the best examples they can be for their kids and talking with their kids about difference, diversity, and bias before challenging situations arise. But even then, our kids are likely to be victims or ob-

> **Hate hurts. Challenging the hate and healing the hurt begins at home.**

servers of biased words or acts and might even stumble themselves and be perpetrators of them. In Part Two, we'll provide you with specific ways to handle situations we hope will never happen to your child.

Questions About Hate

Responses to Hate

Introduction

Both parents and children have questions about hate. While the language used to frame these questions differs greatly between these two groups, the questions themselves are very similar in content. When hate strikes, both parents and children want to know, "Why did this bad thing happen?" "Why did it happen to me?" "What can I do about this hateful situation?" And they ask, "How can I prevent this from happening again?"

From Part One we learned that questions arise in two ways: in preparing and educating kids and in responding to challenges they face. In Part Two we explore the many questions hate makes us pose both in the everyday process of rearing our children and in the truly tough beyond-everyday situations. The former questions are arranged developmentally, from birth to the teens. The latter ones are grouped by topic, from seemingly innocuous name-calling or joking around to systematic taunting and teasing. In both approaches, we explore the questions children and parents most often ask, and we offer a range of responses for a variety of situations.

As you read Part Two, please keep in mind the following points:

◆   There is no "one size fits all" response for hate situations.

◆   As with learning most things, practice brings an increased comfort level and expertise.

The topics explored are complex. Sometimes it's hard to distinguish the so-called "good guys" from the "bad guys." Nowhere is that more true than when our own children are the perpetrators of hate speech and behavior. We always love them, but we ask ourselves, "How can this beloved child of mine be doing this?" "What does this say about me as a parent?" Take a deep breath. Parents can't fix every situation, but there are strategies for assisting our children when they are the perpetrators of hate, and there are steps that can be taken in advance to de- crease the likelihood that children will target others.

Hate undermines the physical and emotional well-being of individuals, families, communities, and society at large. No one is untouched when hate incidents occur. As a society, we must both educate ourselves so that we recognize hate behavior in all its manifestations and not wait for it to escalate before we address it seriously. These questions and answers are an important beginning.

Especially for Families

- **Teach your children about your family, culture, and community. Help your children to take pride in their heritage.**

- **Promote diversity. Stress that differences between people make life more interesting.**

- **Encourage your children by praising their accomplishments.**

- **Give children opportunities to solve problems and make decisions.**

- **Spend time with your children doing things you all enjoy.**

- **Listen carefully to your children without judging or criticizing. Show that you respect and trust them.**

- **Select books, toys, and movies that present all cultural groups accurately and sensitively.**

- **Point out to your children when an ethnic or racial group is stereotyped on television or in a book. Tell children that it is not fair to stereotype. Explain why the stereotypes are inaccurate, then encourage discussion.**

- **Remind children that racist, anti-Semitic, homophobic, or sexist jokes — even when told by friends, relatives, or on television — are hurtful.**

- **Remind children to create positive change. Talk to them about how they can respond to prejudiced thinking or acts of discrimination when they observe them (for example, painting over racist graffiti, writing letters to a television or radio program).**

- **Remember that you are a role model. Children watch what you do more carefully than they listen to what you say.**

- **Take appropriate action against prejudice and discrimination. Your children need to know that discriminatory behavior is unacceptable; children will look to adults to learn how to confront bigotry.**

CHAPTER 5

Hello, World: Questions and Answers for Infants to Preschoolers

A s we showed in Chapter 1, children enter the world like sponges, soaking up all that surrounds them. Because they can't move themselves around or formulate concrete thoughts to make sense out of what they are soaking up, they are completely dependent upon those who provide for their needs. Security is established if they learn to trust that caregivers will feed them when they're hungry, change them when they're wet, place them so that they are comfortable, and make sure they are surrounded by interesting things to see, hear, and feel. They are developing their sensory capacities at this stage, and while it is important not to overwhelm them, they have a great thirst for stimulation. Make that stimulation as diverse as you can.

In the toddler stage, our little sponges begin to take on their worlds. Crawling and later walking, our children begin to explore their environments more independently. Exposure to diverse touches, smells, tastes, and sights in the early part of children's lives creates a larger comfort zone with a wide variety of things.

At around age two, the favorite activity of toddlers is to ask why. Their questions can cause embarrassment or exasperation, but remember that at no other time do our brains absorb as much as they do in our first few years of life. Each time we answer that "why?" we shape our child's attitudes toward differences later in life. It is during this stage that we are often asked about basic physical differences. Here are some examples of appropriate and inappropriate responses to questions that frequently come out of the mouths of our two- to three-year-olds:

"Why does Lee sound so funny when he talks?"

Appropriate Response: *"I am sure that the way Lee speaks sounds different to you. It is different from the way you speak. There is a reason for that. People who learn another language first often say words a* *bit differently from those people who learn English first. Lee is Chinese. His mom and dad speak Chinese and they taught Lee to speak Chinese. It is great to speak more than one language, don't you think? Maybe Lee will teach us how to say a few words in Chinese. If you don't understand what Lee is saying, it is okay to ask him to say it again or to explain it in a different way. But it is not a good idea to say that he is speaking 'funny.' He is just speaking 'differently' from the way you speak. Saying 'funny' might hurt his feelings, and we wouldn't want to do that."*

In this answer, you have helped your child understand what makes Lee's language sound different and have shown that it is not a negative by pointing out the advantage that Lee has in knowing what your child does not know. You have provided your little one with some guidance on how to act in the future, giving him the reasons behind the behaviors you are asking for.

Inappropriate Response: *"Lee can't help how he speaks. Just pretend you don't notice it."*

By saying this, you imply that your child is correct in his description, that Lee does speak "funny."

You also imply that something is wrong with Lee and that the polite thing to do is to pretend not to notice the way Lee speaks. This sends a further message to your child. It subtly tells him that English as it is commonly spoken in America is superior and that any other way of speaking it is wrong. Finally, it fails to answer the question; it does not provide the explanation your child is seeking for the reason behind the difference.

"Is Pamela's skin brown because she is dirty? Will it wash off?"

Appropriate Response: *"People's skin comes in all different colors. Some people are a darker shade than others. This is not dirt and it does not wash off. People are born with their skin color. Pamela's skin is brown like her mommy and daddy's skin."*

This answer provides your child with specific information and also propels her to consider how the answer might apply to other situations. Today your child has noticed that Pamela is different from her. Tomorrow your child may notice another skin color and will know the answer.

Inappropriate Response: *"We are all the same color underneath the skin. It doesn't matter that Pamela is brown."*

Your child has asked for specific information. This answer fails to provide it. It implies that noticing differences is bad and that differences themselves are bad. By asking our child to ignore Pamela's skin color, you imply that it is not worth noticing. Pamela's skin color reflects a rich heritage. It is worth noticing and certainly is not bad.

"Why don't that man's legs work?"

Appropriate Response: *"Perhaps he was in an accident or had a disease that left his legs not working. I bet he has to find other ways to do some things that we don't even think about when we do them, huh?"*

This answer again provides the specific information the child is asking for and helps the child to see the whole person, not just his or her disability.

Bear in mind that some children are afraid of illnesses and may think that if a person has had an illness or an accident it may in some way be contagious. If this is the case with your child, you might want to add information to allay this fear.

Inappropriate Response: *"Shhh. I don't know why, but don't worry about it. It isn't nice to notice people's handicaps."*

This type of answer silences your child without providing information. Instead of educating your child, it implies that the question itself was wrong, stifling your child's growing mind. Also, many people find the term "handicapped" offensive when used to describe a person, preferring instead to focus on the person first, as in "a person with a disability."

The key to answering questions at this stage of your child's life is making sure she has the most exposure possible to diversity so that the questions will be asked naturally as part of everyday life.

CHAPTER 6

Watch Out, Here I Come:
Questions and Answers for Three- to Five-Year-Olds

P reschoolers begin to interact with the outside world, and for the first time they may do so without a parent or primary caregiver constantly by their side. As their world becomes more complex, so do their questions. They accept that there are differences in gender, speaking styles, abilities, and skin color.

And they are beginning to explore where they fit into this social construct. As preschoolers begin to form their first friendships, they become more aware of differences beyond the purely physical. They notice the traditions and celebrations of others, as well as those of their family. They notice the various shades of skin color. They discover the talents and abilities of those who surround them.

Their first friends may have great influence on their thinking. It is not unusual to have a preschooler respond to questions about why he thinks a certain way with, "Well, that's what Sean thinks." "I like the yellow candies because they're Sean's favorites — and we're best friends." Help your children to see that they can disagree and still remain friends. Teach your child how to comfortably say, "Wow, Susie! That is great that you like the red ones. I like the blue ones!" or "You celebrate Kwanza? Wow! We celebrate Chanukah!" Such interaction goes a long way toward teaching them to respect differences without relinquishing their individuality.

Another way to do this is to help them make a list of things they like to do that mommies, daddies, and caregivers might not, and vice versa. Talk about the fact that even though you love one another, you do not always have the same likes and dislikes. Discuss how you and your partner have differences. "Daddy loves to spend his time out in the yard gardening, while I prefer a good run and then plopping down in the chair." Or "Mommy always orders pizza and I always order spaghetti."

First Stereotypes

arents and caregivers need to be alert to early signs of stereotyping and biased thinking. Children at this age may be starting to form unconscious stereotypes on which they base their likes and dislikes. Understand that three- to five-year-olds often are incapable of expressing why they feel a certain way about something. They just do not know. Directly asking a child this age why will usually draw a response like, "I forget why." Yet it may still be helpful to look for "whys" with the child. Brainstorm reasons and alternatives with him or her and then see if any resonate.

For example, when your child states, "Only _____ people are good people," you might ask one of the following questions and give your child time to thoughtfully reply: "What makes _____ people good? What are some things that _____ people can do? Are some of your friends _____? Did someone tell you that only _____ people are good? Did something happen at school, on the playground, at home, or on TV that makes you think that only _____ people are good?" This will help you identify why your child believes what he or she is saying and will help you to formulate your response.

Another necessary step you will need to take if children are beginning to form a stereotype is to help them explore why the stereotype is not true. Ask these questions: "Do you know _____ people? Have you ever seen any bad _____ people? Have you known other kinds of people who are good? Bad?" Help your child arrive at the conclusion that his or her statement just doesn't hold up.

Understanding the harm of stereotypes and how they lead to discrimination are big concepts, and it may take some time for the child to grasp them. But this is a good age at which to point out why it is important not to make general statements about a group of people. Point out that each of us is unique. Television, books, and other forms of entertainment often provide the basis for discussions about prejudice and bias. It is important to let your preschoolers know that it is wrong to stereotype. The questions above provide them with the critical thinking skills you want them to develop. If these skills are practiced, your child will then learn to do this on his or her own in other situations.

Below are a few examples of the types of conversations you might have with your child during this stage:

"Why don't people like those people?"

Appropriate Response: *"Some people have opinions about a whole group of people without knowing very much about them. How can you like or dislike someone you don't even know? It isn't good or smart to think that just because people look similar they all act a certain way."*

This is a good response because it explains why people resort to certain behaviors and is direct in informing your child that this behavior is wrong. It reinforces what are good and bad behaviors, which this age group is very concerned with.

Inappropriate Response: *"They're prejudiced. You have to learn to get along with everyone."*

This response uses terms that are likely to be beyond your child's comprehension and says the attitude is bad without truly explaining either the correct or incorrect attitude.

"Why do people call them names?"

Appropriate Response: *"Sometimes people are afraid of those who seem different from them, and unfortunately, that fear can make them behave badly. They might start name-calling or treat those people meanly. Name-calling is wrong. It hurts people. Do you think the people who do the name-calling know all of the people who look a certain way?"*

This response provides a clear, direct answer, naming the incorrect behavior and explaining why it is incorrect.

Inappropriate Response: *"'Sticks and stones can break my bones but names will never harm me.' Forget about it; name-callers are stupid."*

This response fails to answer the question or to point out what is right and what is wrong. It only serves to silence the questioner. It implies that words do not hurt, when in fact they do. Research has shown us that hate escalates. It starts with words and then can grow to violence. Your child should not tolerate or perpetrate name-calling.

Children need to know that this is unacceptable behavior and that you will not tolerate it.

Preschoolers are learning new ways to express themselves. During this period, many children test out new attitudes and behaviors, usually mimicking someone or following the lead of an adult. Our children begin to define their own thoughts as separate from the thoughts of others. They need help now in learning to be sensitive to the feelings of others as they negotiate their own feelings and meet their own needs. This is a pivotal time to shape values before they head off to school.

CHAPTER 7

Onward and Upward:
Questions and Answers for Six- to Eight-Year-Olds

A s our children march off to elementary school, their worlds greatly expand. Watching our babies go off to "big school," we long to put something in their packs that will protect them from experiencing any pain. A great tool we can provide is knowledge that will help them not only to negotiate the many differences they will encounter but also to feel pride in the ways in which they will be perceived as different.

> **Watching our babies go off to 'big school,' we long to put something in their packs that will protect them from experiencing any pain.**

For many children, the start of formal school will coincide with their first exposure to prejudice. The extent to which you have prepared them will go a long way toward helping them get through

it and respond to it. Before school starts, set aside
time to have a conversation with your child about
differences. Start by making sure that your child has
the correct vocabulary for the discussion.

Big Words for Little Kids

DEFINITIONS FOR AGES SIX TO NINE

For younger children, it is not essential that the
terms stereotype, prejudice, discrimination, and
scapegoating be used. It is important, however,
that the concepts be discussed. This can be done
by using simpler language and explanations. Discuss the following behaviors with children and
whenever possible, provide clear examples for
clarification. Since these words are often used in
daily life, your child may already know them. If so,
be sure she understands the meaning of them so
she can use them correctly.

Stereotype (an idea)

Example: "All four-year-olds are crybabies."

Sometimes we look at groups of people and think
they are all the same in one way or another. We
think that everyone in a group is the same as

everyone else. We need to remember that each person is an individual. We are all different from one another and thereby special for that reason alone.

Prejudice (a feeling)

Example: "I hate four-year-olds."

Sometimes we feel and think about people and things in an unfair way. We often have these thoughts and feelings because we are unfamiliar with the people or things we have negative feelings about. Everyone feels and thinks this way sometimes; it means we have more to learn about people and things.

Discrimination (an action)

Example: "We don't play with four-year-olds."

There are many times when we treat another person or a group of people unfairly and this can hurt their feelings. Sometimes we act this way because of a stereotype or prejudice. Sometimes we are hurtful and we do not know it. Either way, we have to learn not to be hurtful.

Scapegoating (an action)

Example: "Let's blame the mess in the playroom on the four-year-olds because we don't want to get in trouble."

Sometimes we blame others for things that are not actually their fault. We may do this because we have a stereotype or prejudice about them.

Review previous discussions and agreements you've already reached about what is acceptable or unacceptable behavior. Ensure that your child understands that it is a firm rule that no person should be teased or excluded because of what he or she looks like or because of the faith that he or she practices or the way that he or she speaks.

Talk a bit about what your child will do if someone does or says something to hurt her. Encourage your child to speak up and share these occurrences with you. Point out your role as a helper.

Now that your child will be going out into the world without you, often he will not be able to reach out to you in the moment that he is seeking a response to name-calling or taunting. Role-play the possible scenarios below and come up with responses. If your child is called a name, what might the response be? Practice saying things such as, "Don't call me that," "That's not fair," or "You don't like being called bad names and neither do I."

Sample Scenarios

elect one or more of the following scenarios to help you talk with your child about how to respond to hurtful situations. Read the scenario together and use these questions to guide your discussion:

◆ What is the conflict?

◆ What are the different points of view of the people involved?

◆ How do you think the people involved in the situation felt?

◆ What are possible fair solutions to the conflict?

Name-calling

James is a new boy at school and is just beginning to make friends. The group of boys that he is getting to know are always calling people names. James doesn't like to hear people called these names, but he doesn't want to lose his new friends.

Scapegoating

Luanne is the youngest of seven children in her working-class family. She always wears hand-me-down clothes to school. Lately, there has been a great deal of stealing from the children's desks — lunch money, small games, and pens. People begin to spread a rumor that Luanne is taking the items, even though there is no evidence that she is.

Discrimination

David, Jamal, and Michael are planning a basket-ball game for after school and would like a fourth player. Jackie volunteers because she really enjoys playing basketball and is friends with the boys. The boys, however, quickly tell her she can't play because she is not strong enough or fast enough to play with them. Jackie accuses the boys of not letting her play just because she is a girl. Their response is that she just can't keep up with them and therefore can't play.

Prejudice

Ming is the only Asian student in the class. Some of her classmates tease her because they think her family eats funny foods like seaweed. Karen stands up for Ming to tell the other children to stop teasing her, but they begin to ridicule her, too.

It is important for your child to know that he or she always has options when a conflict occurs. As you go through the sample scenarios and think about possible responses, consider each of the options described below:

1. **Listen actively to each other's side of the conflict.** Paraphrase what the other person says. Reflect on what you did and why.

2. **Ignore the problem and walk away.** Sometimes it is not worth arguing, especially when violence may occur. Don't think of yourself as a "scaredy-cat." You are doing the right thing.

3. **Ask questions.** Sometimes conflicts arise because of misunderstanding. Make sure you understand each other.

4. **Ask for help.** It is okay to ask someone to help in mediating a conflict or to help you communicate with another person. Ask an adult whom you trust to be fair to help resolve a conflict.

5. **Compromise.** Talk it out and say how you feel and what you need. It is important to be fair and respectful in listening to what the other person has to say.

6. **Take responsibility for your actions and your words.** Give the other person the respect that you would want, and be fair.

When discussing problem solving with six- to eight-year-olds, remember that they will most likely want to have an active role for themselves in the solution. While they may not be able to change the mind of a perpetrator, it will help if they can be part of proving the perpetrator is not correct or in teaching others why hate hurts.

Sample questions you might typically hear from six- to eight-year-olds are:

"Today at recess, the boys said I couldn't play basketball because I'm a girl and only boys play ball. It isn't fair."

Appropriate Response: *"I am sorry that happened. I bet it made you feel pretty bad, huh? And maybe even a little angry? Lots of girls play basketball. Let's get tickets to the next WNBA game. Do you think you'd like to invite some of those boys to see for themselves what good players girls can be?"*

This answer first acknowledges that the adult is concerned with what happened and is sympathetic to how it must have felt to be denied an opportunity to do something the child wanted to do. Further, it puts a plan in place whereby the young girl can take a positive action against an obvious stereotype.

Inappropriate Response: *"Don't worry about it. The boys were probably just worried that you would beat them."*

Responses that start with "don't worry about it" dismiss the question's significance. By making a derogatory remark about the boys, you are not teaching appropriate behaviors but rather saying that it is okay to make such remarks.

"Today Timmy from next door wanted to play with me but I said no. I hate all four-

year-olds. They're babies. His mom was sure
mad. Do I have to play with him?"

Appropriate Response: *"Sometimes we feel and
think about people in an unfair way. This might
lead us to treat another person unfairly, and this
can hurt their feelings.*

*"Remember when we talked about stereotypes?
We agreed that it was wrong to look at groups of
people as all the same. All four-year-olds are not the
same, so can you hate all four-year-olds? Is there
something about Timmy that you do not like? Is
there a reason besides his age that makes you not
want to play with him? I know that the last time the
two of you played together you had a lot of fun.
However, you may choose who you want to play
with and who you do not want to play with, as long
as you aren't making your decisions because of a
stereotype and as long as you are not hurtful toward
the person asking you to play.*

*"When you said that, you hurt Timmy's feelings,
which is why his mommy was angry. If you didn't
feel like playing with Timmy today, what else might
you have said that would not have been hurtful?
What can you do now to let Timmy know you're
sorry for hurting him?"*

This is an appropriate response because it reviews what you've already discussed, points out the inappropriate behavior, and lets the child make recommendations for both future behavior and for correcting the error he committed today. It also asks your child to identify if there is a legitimate reason why he might not want to play with Timmy. This is important because respecting differences does not require that everyone like everyone else. We can all show respect without liking a particular person. Liking and disliking are personal choices. Respect is mandatory.

Inappropriate Response: *"That's terrible. We don't act that way. You march yourself over to Timmy's house right now and apologize."*

This approach denies your child the explanation he is seeking and only serves to close him off from approaching you again in the future. It does not allow your child to accept any responsibility for his or her actions, either in the initial behavior or in how it will now be handled. Forced apologies rarely are delivered with genuine contrition. Instead, they become meaningless words that often further anger the offender.

Six- to eight-year-olds are entering the world outside their home. They may face prejudice for the first time, but they are also better able to understand the concept and develop skills to deal with it. They are sensitive to issues of fairness and can learn basic ways to resolve conflicts. They look to adults for examples of appropriate behavior. This is the beginning of their search for their own values.

CHAPTER 8

Tweens: Questions and Answers for Nine- to Twelve-Year-Olds

Preteens, or "tweens," are testing out what they perceive to be more adult behaviors as they formulate the basic moral codes that will take them into adulthood. They begin to understand how cultural values develop and how they affect different groups of people. They question and requestion their own emerging values against the values of the adults around them and the communities and institutions to which they belong. Instead of just wanting to copy adult behavior and attitudes, they now want to know the reasons for them.

This can be a scary time for parents. Our children no longer assume "we know everything" and instead begin a "values" shopping trip. As they try on new designer fashions, we hope they retain some of the tried-and-true styles.

When our children look in the mirror to decide what "fits," they sneak a look at our faces to see what our opinions are. They sneak a look as well at friends, teachers, and others. Tweens are stuck between dependence and independence, between establishing who they are and trying to fit in. They are mature enough to discern their own preferences but are not equipped to exercise them without our help. For example, they know they want to go to the mall, but they can't yet drive themselves there. They know they want to attend that concert, but on their own they can't afford the tickets or have our permission to stay out so late. And they may have their own feelings about those who are different from them but are not yet able to navigate relationships in keeping with their views.

> **When our children look in the mirror to decide what 'fits,' they sneak a look at our faces to see what our opinions are.**

We must be ready to explain our own beliefs and offer a safe harbor to these nine- to twelve-year-olds before they enter the stormy seas of the teenage years. Kids this age often feel powerless and need our assurances to empower them to test their own solutions to the challenges they face. This is a time when parents can help their children make their own decisions. The resulting autonomy the kids feel enhances their self-image and self-confidence. They will feel better about themselves if, instead of answers when they raise questions, they receive

◆ respect for what they are saying,

◆ perceptive listening that shows understanding, and

◆ reflective responses that give them the opportunity to clarify their meanings.

Clarifying Values

It is important that you can honestly identify for your tweens your own values and how you arrived at them. This signals that it is safe for them to scrutinize your values and explore their own developing viewpoints. Do you remember particular events that had an impact on shaping your values? Did you disagree with some of your parents' values? How did you deal with those disagreements?

"Every Sunday, for as long as I could remember, I dragged my sorry butt out of bed at 7 A.M. and went with my mom and dad to 8 A.M. Mass. I never thought about it — I just went. I'd sit there during the prayers and plan the rest of my day. I'd think about riding my bike; going into town; seeing the guys; you know, doing regular stuff. One day, my buddy Charlie asked me why I go to church. You know, it hit me hard — I'd never really thought about why. I knew it meant a lot to my mom that I go, but I had never really thought about what it meant to me. Was it important? Did I value it?"

Share your reflections with your children. Let them know that you expect them to examine your values closely and disagree with some, but that you will always discuss them sincerely.

One way to open such a discussion is to participate in a formal values-clarification exercise. You needn't wait until a situation arises to undertake this activity. You can make a game of it. One evening at dinner, ask your children and others at the table to think of the ten things they most like to do. Share your lists with one another, examining patterns that exist. For example, do most items require planning? Involve risks? Cost money? Require others or require being alone? Involve the family? Have a spiritual bent? Involve teaching or learning? Talk about the patterns and see if they help clarify the underlying values upon which each of you operates. Discuss and explore this with one another.

Ask, Don't Tell and Other Protocol

This is a pivotal time in ensuring that your adult-to-be values diversity and understands the need to stand up to hate. In your child's earlier years, your primary role in her values development was as inculcator or modeler. Now you shift to a role that allows your child to make some decisions herself. You are now helping your child decide, not making the decision for her.

This involves asking relevant questions, being a good listener, encouraging self-knowledge, and demonstrating trust in your child's ability to find the answer. Support him as he arrives at his own conclusions. Keep your general lines of communication open by posing questions for reflection and discussion as opposed to preaching.

Respect your young person's peer-group behavior codes. Often this means allowing your child to dispense with public shows of affection and adopt an appearance of greater independence when he is with his friends. Jean-Paul Sartre said, "I leave myself open to all contradiction." It's a good rule to apply to your tween's seemingly contradictory actions when he is out in the world or among his friends as opposed to when he is

> **Accept that he'd rather be dead than hug you when you pick him up from school, but that he still craves a private hug.**

home with family. Accept that he'd rather be dead than hug you when you pick him up from school, but that he still craves a private hug. Act accordingly in each situation.

If his public peer codes reflect values about diversity that you do not agree with or, worse, are indicative of bias, demonstrate your own values in public. This allows your child to view your behavior critically and have space to be his own person without feeling "coerced" into acting out your values. In private, discuss the situations in earnest with your child, even if he wishes to avoid the discussion, as in this scenario:

"I noticed when I picked you up from the movies this afternoon that you didn't even say hi to Jodie when I did as we drove by her."

"So, do I have to do everything you do?"

"You and Jodie used to go to the movies together all the time. It's great that you've made new friends, but I just wonder what happened to you and Jodie."

Silence.

"Well, I just wonder if there is something she did that should make me change the way I relate to her. If she did, maybe I can help in some way."

"Don't you get it? She's white!"

"And . . ."

Silence.

"So she doesn't fit in with your black friends, huh?"

"Yeah, yeah. And she never would have seen me if you hadn't said hello to her! Jodie's always been cool with me. I feel really

**bad dissing Jodie. We've been friends so long,
but, well . . ."**

**". . . but it's different when the black kids
are hanging out?"**

"You know what I'm sayin'."

**"I've had to make choices in balancing
my black and my white friends. I guess I
have decided that ignoring one friend for the
sake of another is not for me. I like Jodie, so I
hope you'll respect the fact that I'm going to
say hi to her when I see her."**

Respecting your child's peer-group protocol and
teaching her to value diversity is a special challenge
at this age because your child's sense of having authority over her own world is associated with in-
group rules. In many cases today, peer-group
pressure is positive. Bias is often considered "wack"
as youth culture becomes more and more multicultural. But if you need to counter such influences —
and you can only counter, not eliminate them —
begin by:

◆ giving your tween more power inside the family circle. Let him make some of the family decisions

and solve problems regarding daily routines, social and recreational activities, vacations, even some budget matters;

◆ allowing your young person total authority over her leisure time and activities: Because kids have so little free time left after school, other instruction, and family responsibilities, they'll appreciate your respect for the time that is totally their own; don't schedule their time without getting their permission;

◆ relinquishing complete control to your child for how he spends his allowance or earned money.

These steps allow your tween a measure of power and authority so she learns that they need not be wrested from you. It reinforces the model that trust is first given, not earned. An empowered young person who feels trusted will respond as you help her make decisions about diversity and confronting bias.

Asking for Affirmation, Not Answers

ypical diversity comments from this age group usually impart a piece of information and then seek affirmation, such as:

"The guys at school all make fun of the Mexican kids. That's not right, is it? But what can I do?"

"He called me a _____! Can you believe it, Mom? How was I supposed to respond to that?"

"They're so uptight. I didn't mean anything when I used that word. I was just being funny. What do you want from me?"

"Jan and I always played together before. Now she'll only hang out with the other Asian kids. What should I do?"

Direct answers to these questions will likely be rejected like last year's clothing styles. Because most of the diversity-related issues that confront tweens will eventually be decided by their own value systems, you need to help them clarify their thinking so that they can answer their questions for themselves.

In each of the diversity situations described above, our tween is questioning his role in the situation. Start by making sure you understand what happened and how your child is feeling about it:

"Wow — were they teasing all of the Mexican kids or one in particular? What started it? I bet the Mexican kids were pretty upset. It sounds like you are, too, huh?"

"It makes me so angry and hurt when people call people names like that. Is that how you felt? What prompted him to call you that name?"

"It sounds like you really didn't mean to hurt anyone, but apparently you did. It doesn't feel very good to hurt people, even unintentionally, does it?"

"I imagine you really miss hanging out with Jan, huh? Did something happen that makes her no longer feel she can be with people who are different from her?"

Each of these statements assures the tween that you are hearing what he is saying, clarifies what you think you heard, lets the speaker know you are concerned with the impact the situation is having on him, and opens the door for more conversation. In fact, the open-ended questions propel your child to examine the situation again and to discuss it.

The next step is to help your child consider if she wants to take action and if so, what action that might be. Helping your child choose an action or response to the situations mentioned above will require helping her reflect on her values. For example:

"Did you feel it was wrong to make fun of the Mexican kids? What makes you feel that way? If you could do anything at all in this situation, what would you like to do? What obstacles exist that might stop you from doing that? Can you think of other ways to accomplish that goal? If you are not willing to do something in this situation, why not?

What does your action or inaction tell people
about you? Is that the message you want
them to receive?"

Be sure you both agree on the definitions of the
language you're using. Children at this age have developed a more complex understanding of such
terms as stereotype, prejudice, and discrimination.

Confronting Bias

Nine- to twelve-year-olds have a more sophisticated sense of unfairness and prejudice and ways
to respond to conflict. Use the following sample
scenarios and guidelines for discussion to help
your children reflect on the roles people can play in
biased situations and to develop their problem-
solving skills.

A group of friends is sitting together in the cafeteria
when one group member comments on how the
Hmong kids always sit together by themselves, talking
all that "gibberish." Most of his friends laugh at the
comment, but one of the friends is uncomfortable and
says, "You shouldn't make fun of them." Everyone else
just keeps laughing.

A group of friends is going to the local movie theater when the driver parks in a space reserved for people with disabilities. One person in the car mentions that they shouldn't park there, but the driver shrugs it off, saying, "Would you rather miss the beginning of the movie?"

Help your kids define the terms "victim," "perpetrator," "bystander," and "challenger," and ask them to identify the people who play those roles in each of the scenarios. Use the following questions to guide a discussion about how to respond to such situations.

- **What might cause someone to go along with a friend who made a hurtful remark or took hurtful action?**

- **Does a hurtful action still hurt if the "victim" is not present (as in the parking scenario)?**

- **If you observe a biased situation and don't feel comfortable speaking up at the time, are there other ways you can address the situation?**

- **What are some of the possible effects of just being a silent bystander?**

- **What are some of the possible risks of challenging bias?**

- **What factors can help you decide whether to be a bystander or a challenger?**

Tweens are truly in between. They are moving away from unquestioning acceptance of parental values toward constructing a value system of their own. This means they test behaviors. Remember that your primary role at this stage is to offer information and guidance as they make their choices. Provide them with opportunities to test and practice their new values and behaviors. When kids ask questions or, more likely, raise concerns, parents need to reflect back to their children what they think they hear their kids saying before they jump in with advice. This gives kids an opportunity to hear their own thinking stated clearly. It also keeps the doors of communication open, letting kids know that parents want to understand what they feel and are trusting them to make certain decisions.

But remember that they're still young. Perhaps the best support you can give them is to ask, "How can I help?"

CHAPTER 9

I Exist, Therefore I Embarrass You: The Teenage Years

As kids reach their teens, they tend to stop talking to their parents. The challenges of this age are to maintain your own standards in the face of sometimes harsh criticism, to be available to your kids without expecting them to be available to you, to set limits but expect them to be fought against. Sometimes your best conversations will take place in the car as you drive them to their next activity, on the train as you go to work and they head for school, or at 1 A.M. in the living room when they aren't tired yet and you happen to wake up from a deep sleep to find them ready to chat. At such moments, remember how rare these conversations can be and take full advantage!

This is not the point in your child's life where you are likely to be asked direct questions or hear a "yes" to the question, "Want to hear what I think?" That does not release you from the responsibility of sharing your thoughts, expecting appropriate behaviors, challenging your teenager to clarify his values, or developing his abilities to value differences and stand up to hate. It is crucial that you let your teenager know what you think, even if he doesn't want to hear it.

Teenagers are likely to seek concrete actions for injustices. A solid first step in this process is to assist your children in honing their conflict resolution skills. Typically, conflict is characterized by three elements:

◆ interdependence

◆ interaction

◆ incompatible goals

Conflict is the interaction between interdependent people who perceive differences in or threats to their needs, their resources, or their values. There are different types of conflict:

◆ Internal conflict — a conflict that occurs within oneself.

> **"I don't know what to do. I don't like how my friends were teasing that gay guy, but I**

**don't want them to think *I'm* gay or that I
don't have a sense of humor."**

◆   Interpersonal conflict — a conflict among two
or more people.

> **"Janine thinks it's okay for the white kids
> to feel like they own the school since we
> were there first. I don't think she's right,
> though; we're all here now."**

◆   Intragroup conflict — a conflict within a group
(groups can be institutions, organizations, any
group of people who share a specific role or identity).

> **"Most of the club members think having
> our big party on Friday night is great . . .
> but the Jewish members don't."**

◆   Intergroup conflict — a conflict among two or
more groups.

> **"The captains of the varsity teams want
> our mascot to be an Indian chief. The Na-
> tive American club is strongly against it."**

Our children encounter conflicts every day. How
they respond to them depends on how well we've

prepared them for the task. Kids can generally respond to conflict in one of three ways: avoidance, confrontation, or communication. Our task is to help them choose the most effective response to the situation.

Responses to Conflict

Responses to conflict generally fall into one of three categories: soft responses, hard responses, or principled responses.

Soft responses involve avoidance. People avoid conflict by withdrawing from the situation, ignoring the problem, or denying their feelings. Avoiding conflict may help in the short run. For instance, it might help someone prevent losing his or her temper. However, avoidance usually causes self-doubt and makes a person feel anxious about the future. In addition, because the conflict is never brought up, it can never be resolved.

Hard responses involve confrontation. Confrontation means a person expresses anger, verbal or physical threats, or aggression. It may also mean the person resorts to bribery or to punishments like withholding money, favors, or affection. These actions show a win–lose attitude toward conflict, or the attitude that one person must win and the other person must lose in a conflict. This attitude prevents cooperation and keeps people from reaching a mutually satisfying solution.

Principled responses involve communication. The parties may not agree but participate in a common understanding. In order for people to cooperate, they must first communicate. People in conflict who first seek to understand the other person's side and then be understood produce win–win solutions.

Even though your child is now older and conflict resolution will play a large part in dealing with her concerns, you will still need to employ the skills discussed previously — clarifying issues, checking out what she is talking about and how she is feeling about it, and discussing alternative responses. Resist solving the problem for her, unless her personal safety is at risk. Help her discern the values she possesses that bring the issue to the foreground, identify what conflicts exist and how they might be managed, and decide how she can go beyond the individual situation to change any overall systemic problem that might be causing it.

Active listening is a key skill for parents at this stage, especially since kids aren't talking to us as

much. Often teenagers' remarks about their conflicts don't at first reveal the questions they have.
Draw out the sometimes hidden issues by addressing
your child's feelings and helping him define the
concern at the root of them. As in the examples
here, you'll find the concern often has to do with
verifying the teenager's perspective and finding an
effective course of action:

**"The white kids think they own the school.
They treat us like we're just visitors spending
some uninvited time there.** *I can't change that,
can I?"*

**"I am sick and tired of waiting until 6 P.M.
when the boys varsity basketball team fin-
ishes practicing so our girls team can get on
the courts.** *It isn't fair, is it?"*

**"He's gay, Mom — it gives me the creeps.
Sure, we've been friends for years, but now
all I can think about is whether or not he
might hit on me and it disgusts me.** *What can
I do?"*

"Why should I even bother applying for that job? You know they're gonna give it to a minority kid. They won't even consider me. *Isn't it a waste of my time?*"

Teenagers, as we have said, are not looking for direct answers from you but rather the opportunity to discover the answers for themselves based on their rapidly solidifying values. They don't want you to "drive" them to their solution; they want you to give them a map so they can know the different directions they might take; they want tools to decide for themselves their own route. They want your assurance that they can find their own way and have an impact on the situations they face.

Your response to your teenager's concerns is a *process* of exploration that involves:

◆   clarifying what your child has said to be sure you've heard the question he needs to answer;

◆   letting your child know you've understood the question;

◆   addressing your child's feelings about the situation;

◆ soliciting and offering options for taking action;

◆ allowing your child to find her own solution;

◆ helping your child identify allies who might also be able to help.

To play out a pattern of response, let's revisit the scenario from the beginning of Chapter 3:

"We had had a number of conversations about the Civil Rights Movement and even about what his grandparents had experienced in the late fifties. But nothing prepared me for my son's sophomore year. It started out great. He made the varsity basketball team and even started in the second game. He had a group of friends and seemed truly comfortable and happy. One week I noticed he was a bit quieter than usual. By the weekend, his silence was deafening. I was surprised to find him home on Saturday evening instead of out with his group of guys. I asked him where everyone was and he told me Lisa M. was having a party. She had initially invited him but on Monday told him

she had to uninvite him. She liked him and was really sorry, but her parents thought it was wrong to have him there. He quoted her final statement: 'After all, people should only date their own kind and a party might lead to dating.' And then he added, 'I thought we were friends, Dad.'"

"Son, this must be really hard for you. I know it would upset me a lot to be excluded from something all of my friends were doing. Has this ever happened before? When she said that to you, what did you say? Were you able to discuss this with any of your other friends?"

You've opened the discussion by addressing how your son is feeling and by expressing your empathy for his situation. He needs to be reassured. He has been delivered a cruel injustice. He's been excluded unfairly. Asking him to tell you about what he said to Lisa enables him to replay the conversation so that together the two of you can discuss alternative options for how he might have responded, as well as for how he might respond in future situations.

Asking if he's discussed this with other friends is

another important question. Many teenage males will not discuss these situations with their male friends. They are just not comfortable showing emotional distress in general, and this will only be compounded if the victim is one of very few people with his background in his peer group. He is experiencing something that his friends most likely are not experiencing. However, you can help him explore how he might share what he is feeling with his friends. If they are his friends, they will be concerned with how he is feeling and what he is experiencing. Perhaps you can start by identifying with him the one person in whom he feels he can most easily confide. It is important that our teenagers develop allies and understand the power of allies.

A fable tells of a father who bundles up ten sticks, binding them together with string. He brings his ten sons to the room and asks that each of them take a turn trying to break the bundled sticks into two. Each son tries but fails. The father then unties the sticks, gives each son one, and again asks that they break the sticks. Each son easily breaks the stick that has been given to him. The moral learned from this fable is that while individually we may break easily, together we cannot be broken. The second message is that if we are to accomplish a difficult task, it is helpful to have allies. The young man in our scenario needs to know he is not in this alone. A parent can help devise a plan to form these important alliances.

You cannot change the fact that Lisa has excluded your son. Do not plan to take action yourself without his explicit permission since his safety is not in question. Keeping the lines of communication open and trusting that together you and your son can arrive at a course of action that he is comfortable with and able to follow through on is more important than engineering a rescue operation. You can only work with him to figure out what he will do about it and reassure him of his own worth. He might decide to work toward eradicating the hate that is behind Lisa's parents' request that he not be invited to the party, or he might decide it is not a challenge on which he chooses to take action.

Often those whose race, religion, culture, or class are different from the majority of people in their community feel burdened by the task of responding to bias. It is not a task they exclusively "own." Make sure your son understands that he can in good conscience choose to handle this biased act by avoiding it if that is most comfortable to him. His jobs are schoolwork, basketball, and his other priorities, and he need only take on this "job" of fighting bias if he chooses. If he chooses to do so, consider what the real conflict is and discuss ways to approach it. Think about whether or not you have reason to believe that Lisa's parents' actions are representative of the majority of moms and dads in your community. Brainstorm ways in which the parents in the community can come to know the teenagers in the community as individuals, not as representatives of particular minority or majority groups.

❝ Teenagers continue to look to their family and family friends as role models. When asked which category their current role model would be from, more than four out of ten teens listed a family member. ❞

We must teach our teens what we know by serving as the sounding board for their thoughts, applauding their successes, picking them up after their failures, and standing with them as they seek to improve our world.

CHAPTER 10

Name-calling

ticks and stones may break my bones but names will never hurt me!" Parents for many generations have taught their children to chant this as a way to help youngsters cope with the real hurt of name-calling. If parents really believed name-calling didn't hurt, there would be no reason to perpetuate this myth.

"You're a stupid idiot!"
"No, you are! You're a stupid dog breath!"

Name-calling does not have to target a person's culture or ethnicity to be hurtful. Children know that making fun of another's body size, clothing, accent, intelligence, or family members are among the many ways they can hurt someone's feelings. Let children know that *all* name-calling results in hurt feelings and is not acceptable.

Sometimes young children do not know the meaning of the words they use, but they do know that the words will get a reaction from the person to whom they are directed and from any adult within hearing. Children need to be told that, like hitting, biting, and throwing objects, such language can hurt and is not acceptable.

"When you said those words you may have been really upset at something someone else did. Instead of telling her that she did something that you didn't like, you called her a word that is used to hurt people. If you tell her what she did that you didn't like, maybe it will help to change her behavior. Name-calling hurts and doesn't solve the problem."

Talk right away to a child who has been the target of hurtful words. Sometimes parents and other caregivers become so involved with the child who said the hurtful words that the child who has been called the name gets lost in the shuffle. Even when they don't completely understand the meaning of the words, and even when they don't want to show that they feel hurt, children who have been called a discriminatory name can feel devastated. Let children know that it's okay to show their hurt, angry, or dejected feelings when they've been called a name. If left unattended, children who have been called hurtful names may themselves become victimizers. Give your children time and opportunities to express how they are feeling.

"You look sad right now. Sometimes people feel sad when they've been called a hurtful name."

"Mommy, why are those men doing this?"

"My first experience with racism happened when I was on vacation in Louisiana with my mother. We were driving from my aunt's house in a predominantly black area of New Orleans and when we had to pass through Pauline — a predominantly white area — at a red light I noticed a red truck in front of us with a Confederate flag in its window. When the light turned green, the truck didn't move. Three or four young white men got out of the truck and started yelling curses and racial slurs like 'nigger' at all the cars coming from the direction of the black area. The road was

**blocked and we couldn't move. We were
trapped and I was frightened. For the first
time in my life I wished I wasn't black."**

The "why" question is almost impossible for parents to answer. We can't know what motivates other
people to act the way they do; we frequently don't
even know why we ourselves act in certain ways.
But parents need to have responses for children
when they are the targets of hate. Don't avoid your
children's questions, even if you don't know the answer to "why." Your children need to hear your
voice.

Appropriate response: *"Sometimes people say or
do mean things. Those men scared you, didn't they?
They scared me, too. You and I will wait in the car
until it's safe for us to go."*

Simply admitting the hurtfulness of words or actions is a good and truthful starting place. Going on
to explore your children's feelings helps them clarify
their thinking. Questions such as "Those men scared
you, didn't they?" might provide an opportunity for
your child to verbalize his or her own fears.

Let your child know how you are feeling. Children need to know that adults, too, get scared, so

they have models of honest adult decision making. Parents cannot always promise children that everything will turn out fine, but we can reassure them that we will do everything we can to make them safe. Children sense when parents are making false assurances, and usually they are not comforted by such statements.

"Why do they hate us so?"

"A few years ago during a workshop for high schools, I asked the hundred or so teenagers in the room to write on a piece of paper the names of groups (not individuals) in the school who were picked on by other students or socially ignored. As I was tabulating the students' responses, I was assisted by a Japanese-American student whose face registered increasing sadness as she saw the word 'JAP' written over and over on the students' papers. She turned to me and said: 'Why do they hate us so?'"

Appropriate response: *In this case, the racial epithets were written and anonymous, but it was clear from the students' responses that to be a "JAP" in that school was not considered a good thing. Ironically,* *the student who felt targeted in this situation was mistaken; the word "JAP" was a pejorative reference to "Jewish-American Princess." When I explained this to the student, she brightened briefly before she asked: "But why do they hate the Jews so much?"*

"Sometimes people call other groups names just to make themselves feel better or stronger, without always realizing how much it hurts."

While the Japanese-American student was visibly relieved to learn that her classmates were not referring to her, the situation allowed her to imagine what the Jewish female students in her school might be feeling. When we help our children develop empathy for others, we decrease the chances that they will victimize others.

"So what? I called him a name. . . ."

"I had the swing first."
"No, I did!"
"No, you always think you have to go first!"
"Fag!"

Appropriate response: *Sometimes children will use hurtful epithets to express their anger without really "meaning" them literally. When we hear our children using such words, it is important for us not to ignore the situation.*

In this situation, two young children are having difficulty sharing. The frustration leads one of the boys to refer to the other as "fag." Even though his words were not referring to the other boy's sexual orientation, it is important to intervene because this language reinforces negative attitudes about homosexuality.

"You just used a word in a way that was meant to be hurtful. Instead of telling José what he did that you didn't like, you called him a name."

Children need to be told explicitly that name-calling of any kind hurts and doesn't solve problems, although they know instinctively that it hurts. That is part of the appeal of using certain words in front of their parents and other adults.

Children often use words they know they shouldn't as an exercise in control. They are fairly sure they'll get some reaction and they want to know just what that reaction will be. Parents' consistency about acceptable and unacceptable language is important. If a parent insists on one code of behavior in public and has another standard for home, a child will rightly perceive the parent's insincerity or, at least, ambivalence about the public

According to a recent research study of the Gay, Lesbian and Straight Education Network (GLSEN), the largest national organization dedicated to ending antigay bias in public, private, and parochial K–12 schools:

- **The average high school student hears antigay epithets 25 times a day.**

- **When teachers hear these comments, they fail to respond 97% of the time.**

- **76% of our nation's schools fail to train teachers about issues facing gay youths.**

- **80% of gay youths report having been verbally abused; these youths are more than four times as likely as their nongay peers to be threatened with a weapon while at school.**

- **Gay youths are more than 5 times as likely as their straight classmates to skip school because they feel unsafe.**

code. "You don't make us do that at home" is a child's likely response to that situation, usually said loudly and publicly.

Children of all ages need to learn that some values and behaviors are nonnegotiable. Respecting oneself and others and not inflicting harm on oneself or others are underlying values behind teaching children about name-calling. Parents must decide which specific words are unacceptable, using the principle of respect for all people.

Sometimes children use hurtful names because they are angry at someone. Teach kids that, while it is okay to be angry, it is not okay to use a hurtful word to retaliate. Children must learn appropriate ways to express their anger without using hurtful words. Effective ways of resolving conflicts are telling the person with whom they are angry why they are angry and discussing possible solutions to resolve the situation.

The best way to teach children effective ways to manage their anger is to model that behavior yourself. If we yell at children in anger and call them hurtful names, they will learn from us to yell and direct hurtful names at others. Remember that your children watch you carefully for cues about handling angry feelings. If you use name-calling in arguments that are witnessed by your children, you are less likely to be successful in stopping their name-calling than if you model a problem-solving approach to conflicts.

What Parents Can Do to Respond to Name-calling

1. Name the behavior when you see it: "What you did was name-calling."

2. Be clear about your expectation: "We don't use those words here." Declare it unacceptable: "We don't call people names."

3. Teach your children the truth about hurtful words: "Name-calling hurts."

4. Help your children examine their actions: "How did you feel when you used those words? Did it make you feel good to say those words? What are some other ways you can feel good about yourself?"

5. Follow through: "We will talk about this." (Specify a time and do it.)

When Your Child Uses Hurtful Names

Older children sometimes use name-calling to define "in" and "out" groups that can create exclusive and hostile environments for children in the "out" groups. Peer pressure increases in teen years and joining the teasing and taunting can be hard to resist. Although name-calling can appear innocuous, especially compared to physical violence, continued name-calling can be very painful; its cumulative impact can have long-lasting effects.

Parents, teachers, clergy, youth leaders, and all adults in children's lives should be prepared to address name-calling when it occurs. Saying or thinking "kids will be kids" and ignoring such behavior can allow it to escalate to extreme proportions. But keep in mind that just because your child called someone a hurtful name does not mean you are a "bad" parent.

Children and young adults need to be taught and reminded that name-calling is unfair. Encourage them to speak up when someone does or says something they do not like, but to do it in a noncombative way. Remind them that name-calling does not resolve conflicts.

SUMMARY OF ADVICE FOR PARENTS WHEN YOUR CHILD IS THE NAME-CALLER

- **Teach your children that name-calling is unfair.**

- **Name the behavior when it occurs: "What you did was name-calling."**

- **Help your children examine their behavior: "How did you feel when you called him a name? Did it make you feel good to say those words?"**

- **Help your children develop positive self-esteem: "What are some other things you can do to feel good about yourself?"**

- **Be clear about your expectations: "We don't use those words because they hurt people's feelings and they don't help solve problems."**

When Your Child Has Been on the Receiving End of Hurtful Words

When your child is the target of name-calling, be prepared to listen carefully to his or her feelings. Sometimes our children are reluctant to tell us when they have been the victim of name-calling because they fear we will overreact. One of the hardest aspects of parenting is allowing our children to have their own feelings separate from our own. It is hard for us to see our children hurt without feeling the pain ourselves. Understandably, we want to fix a situation in which our children have been targeted by hurtful names or actions.

Ask yourself the following questions:

1. Is my child's physical safety an issue in this situation? Note: If you think that is the case, inform all appropriate school and municipal authorities about the situation immediately.

2. Is my child's emotional well-being at risk? What friends or professionals can I call for help with this situation?

3.   Have I created a home environment that encourages my child to share this situation with me? Do I have all of the information I need? If not, how can I get it?

4.   Am I allowing my feelings to get in the way of helping my child? Are there elements of this situation that have triggered an emotional response on my part that may be related to something that happened to me in my own childhood?

5.   Have I given my child the skills to handle this situation? What does my child need from me?

SUMMARY OF ADVICE FOR PARENTS WHEN YOUR CHILD IS THE TARGET OF NAME-CALLING

- **Listen carefully to your child's hurt feelings.**

- **Try not to overreact. Understand that sometimes children are reluctant to tell their parents when they have been called bad names because they don't want to upset their parents.**

- **Help your children develop skills to handle such situations. Involve children in working with you to create some ready-made responses, for example, "Don't call me that — it's not my name."**

CHAPTER 11

Joking

"How many _____s does it take to change a lightbulb?"

The answer to this well-known one-liner depends on what word gets inserted into the blank. Ethnic and other group membership jokes are very popular in schools and workplaces and are also disseminated widely via e-mail.

Ethnic jokes and other "put-down" humor are the subject of considerable controversy. According to some people, humor that uses ethnicity as the basis for its comic thrust is always demeaning and produces emotional harm to the targets of such jokes. Others disagree, arguing that ethnic humor provides a much-needed release of intergroup tension and is generally a harmless source of entertainment and fun.

Both of these views are overly simplistic. All ethnic humor is not the same. We must differentiate ethnic humor based on its function and impact.

Ethnic humor can be positive when it portrays multidimensional characters in common situations. We are encouraged to identify with these characters as they experience the pathos of daily life. When we laugh, we laugh with the characters, affirming our common humanity. In a fundamental sense, positive ethnic humor transcends ethnicity because it provides a universal message with wide human appeal that serves to break down prejudicial stereotypes.

Ethnic humor is negative when it presents stock, one-dimensional characters in stereotypical situations. We are encouraged not to identify with the characters but to see them as objects of derision. Laughter is directed at these characters; we are not laughing with them. By laughing, we are encouraged to feel and affirm our superiority, denying common humanity with the joke's target. Such humor reinforces prejudicial stereotypes and often serves as a weapon of social control.

"My first grader came home from school laughing hysterically with her friends as the

two of them repeated a number of 'blond' jokes they had heard in school that day. I was shocked to hear the kids laughing and repeating these jokes. The jokes were making me uncomfortable, but I couldn't decide if I was being oversensitive because I'm blond (and so is my daughter). I couldn't decide if this was a good moment to stop the joke telling and discuss the harm of telling jokes that put people down. I went into another room out of the hearing of the kids and I never said anything. I wondered later if the jokes had been about a racial or ethnic group if I would have had a clearer sense about what to say or to do."

Responding to prejudicial words and actions in young children, especially when such words are couched as jokes, can be tricky. While we want to give children clear messages about acceptable and unacceptable behavior we also do not want to over-react. Some general hints include the following:

1. Establish behavioral guidelines with your children. Let them know how you feel about jokes and other remarks that make fun of people.

2. Hold yourself to the same standard you expect from your children. If you don't want them to use certain words or tell certain kinds of jokes, be sure you do not use those words or tell those jokes yourself.

3. Let other people in your life know that you are offended when they use words and tell jokes that are insulting so that your children can see you as a positive model of someone who is consistent in beliefs and practice.

4. Whenever possible, respond to incidents of insensitivity when and where they occur.

5. Make sure that your children know that you expect all people to be treated with respect.

6. Model respectful ways of letting others know that their words or actions have offended or hurt you. Responding rudely when you are offended compounds a situation. Starting such conversations with "I" as opposed to "you" lets others know how you feel without blaming and finger-pointing. You have the right to let others know what kinds of humor offend you and to request that such words and jokes not be used in your presence; you don't have

the right to tell others what's funny and what isn't. That is a matter of personal opinion.

7. Understand that children are keenly aware of differences, and they must be taught to understand and respect differences rather than pretending they don't notice them.

8. Keep in mind that, like us, children are not perfect. They will make mistakes, and they will have to be reminded about not using words and telling jokes that demean people, even if the joke is about a group of which your child is a member.

9. Children know what's fair and what's not fair. Develop empathy in your children by asking them to consider how they would feel if they were the target of a "put-down" joke.

10. Teach your children a response they can use so that when they are offended by someone's words or actions they have skills to take action.

"One day last year in school, when I was in the fifth grade, one of the other kids told a joke that made fun of Jews in the Holocaust who were put into ovens. Lots of the kids

laughed at the joke. I didn't think it was funny, and it also made me mad that everyone was laughing at that joke because my grandmother has a number tattooed on her arm from that time. I don't think the Holocaust is something to joke about. The worst part for me was that my teacher heard the joke, too, and she didn't say anything about it. Now those kids think those jokes are okay, and they tell them all the time in front of me. I want to say something, but I don't know what to do."

Here, a simple response such as "I don't think that's funny" or "That joke hurts my feelings" would have allowed this child to express her discomfort, even in the face of her teacher's silence.

We need to help our children develop strategies for intervening when they are offended by jokes. Practice the following process with them.

Responding to Situations You Find Offensive: A Five-step Process

1. Begin by clarifying for yourself what you want to get out of the situation.

2. Try to assume goodwill. Many people who make offensive remarks do so out of ignorance. Because they do not intend harm, they assume no harm is done.

3. Sometimes it helps to talk to the person privately.

4. Start the conversation by letting the person who offended you know that he or she is important to you and that is why you want to have this conversation: "I wanted to talk with you, Mary, because your friendship is important to me . . ."

5. Be honest about your feelings and state them directly. Using the word "I" to start the conservation lets the other person know how you feel without feeling attacked; for example, "I was hurt when I heard what you said about . . ." You have every right

to let someone know how you feel; you do not have the right to dictate what others can or cannot say.

"A few years ago my daughters, then ten and twelve, and I were traveling to Florida on the train. My younger daughter and I were in the club car, eating and talking to people. At one of the tables was a group of people playing cards. One of the men in the group, a white man in his mid- to late twenties, began telling 'jokes' to his companions. Not only was he extremely loud, but his 'jokes' were highly offensive and targeted many groups, including women, Jews, gays and lesbians, African-Americans, and Asian-Americans. I hoped that one of his companions — who included another white man, an African-American man, and an African-American woman — would say something to him about his offensive language and hurtful 'jokes,' but no one did. Other people in the car shook their heads in distaste or disgust and whispered among themselves, but no one spoke up.

"I knew that my daughter was waiting to see what I would do, waiting to see if my behavior on this occasion would reinforce the messages I had been giving her for as long as she could remember about not being silent in the face of injustice and bigotry.

"I finally told the man that I found his jokes very painful to hear. He became very angry and told me that if I didn't like it, I should leave. The other people in his group also told me to mind my own business. Not one of the many other people in the club car echoed my sentiments; in fact, most looked away. I reiterated my feelings, but when it still didn't stop, my daughter and I left.

"I felt that I hadn't been successful in getting the man or his friends to consider how hurtful their actions were and was deeply troubled that no one else in the club car supported me when I spoke up. But later in the evening, when my daughter told me that she was proud of me, I realized that despite my feelings of inadequacy, there was a positive outcome to the situation. My daughter had seen me stand up to bigotry even when the decision was unpopular and unsupported.

"For months afterward, she told everyone

who would listen about that night. She told
the story with great pride, and as her pride
grew, so did mine. I know that someday,
somewhere, there's a good chance that she
will speak out against hatred, even if it's unpopular, even if she's alone. I'm proud that I
taught my daughter that."

"Mommy, why doesn't someone say something?"

When our children see that we have the courage
and conviction to interrupt hateful words, we model
for them the possibility of a fairer, more harmonious world. But in many situations, like the one
above, if someone such as that parent is not present,
no one will speak up. Remind your child that we do
not have full information on the power relationships between the individuals present. If the joker is
the boss or client, the hearer may feel he must just
grin and get paid.

Appropriate response: *"I am wondering the
same thing. Perhaps the others have become so
hardened to these kinds of jokes that they don't let
themselves feel offended. Or maybe they feel there
will be repercussions if they speak up."*

Again, you don't need to have all the answers to your child's questions. You only need an honest response that will provide an opportunity for reflection and insight into differences.

Many people who have faced long-term, systematic oppression have become so accustomed to put-downs that they choose to pick their battles. Compared to economic, judicial, and social injustice, interpersonal joking may be to them a non-issue. But make it clear to your child that it is an issue for you and that you do not approve.

Sexual Orientation and Disability Slurs

Overheard in the hallways of many secondary schools:

"Oh, that was sooooo gay!"

"That exam was really lame."

When teens use the expressions "gay" and "lame," more often than not these words have nothing to do with sexual orientation or physical ability. People who use "gay" and "lame" might be referring to anything, but those listening know that whatever is being referred to is not good. "Gay" and "lame" mean "bad" in this context, even when they are not being used specifically to demean someone's sexual orientation or physical ability.

Teens often strive to find their own language, one that only they can understand, excluding those who don't comprehend their secret jargon. In- and out-group behavior can be very strong during the teen years, fulfilling a need for group belonging as children move emotionally away from their parents and other family members en route to becoming independent adults.

Teens need clear direction from the adults in their lives about what it means to be fair. "Put-down" jokes are not fair. It doesn't feel good to be on the receiving end of such treatment, and teens need to be encouraged to find group membership and belonging within the confines of fairness.

As with all anti-bias teaching, what you do and say is the strongest determinant of your child's

Thoughtful Questions about Jokes

Take the following brief quiz to clarify your thinking about jokes and take time to discuss your thoughts with family and friends.

1. **What messages are conveyed in this joke?**

2. **Who might be offended by this joke?**

3. **What harm might there be in spreading this joke?**

4. **Would I be offended if I were the target of this joke?**

5. **What message is conveyed by laughing at this joke?**

6. **Would this joke be told if a member of the group being targeted in the joke were present?**

7. **If jokes are told about all groups or people, not just one group, is that okay?**

8. **Am I being oversensitive to object to this joke?**

9. **Do I have the right to ruin a good time for others by objecting to this joke?**

10. **Are jokes about some groups, like lawyers for example, okay because lawyers have not been historically discriminated against?**

behavior. Laughter brings levity to the soul. Learn to see the abundant humor in everyday interactions. The more diverse and genuinely respectful we are of one another, the more we will discover what makes us laugh together.

CHAPTER 12

Excluding, Zooing, and Other Inappropriate Behaviors

Excluding

"I remember it as if it were yesterday. All the girls on our street were preparing for their First Holy Communion. Not only were parties being planned, but each one received a new white dress, complete with a veil and everything. That Sunday morning I watched out the window as they took family photographs and headed for their church, looking like little brides. It was one of those times that being the only Jewish girl on the block sure felt terrible. But not nearly as bad as six years later, when one of my girlfriends told me that the mother of the girl I considered my best friend had asked her to get me 'to leave her daughter alone.' It appeared that this woman had high hopes for her daughter that she felt would be undermined by having a Jewish friend. The pain of that day is still with me — 33 years later."

"Most of the kids in my daughter's homogenous middle school come from similar economic backgrounds — basically middle class. However, there are a few students from an area called the Trailer Park. These kids are on government assistance and receive supplies and school lunches for free. Many of these kids also receive tutorial assistance since their skills may not be competitive with the rest of the student body. Consequently, these students are often singled out for bullying and exclusion because their clothing may not be the same designer brands as other children. On this particular day, a young girl was placed in my daughter's homeroom as a transfer student. Immediately, her peers summed her up by her clothing and made certain assumptions. These were confirmed when the teacher made her tell the class where she was from, where she was living now, etc. While she stammered in front of

**her classmates, a group of girls at the back
of the room began to giggle and whisper
about her. . . . Every stereotype reflecting
class issues was made about her. Not one person tried to intervene."**

**"I thought I was doing a great job of raising
bias-free children until my son told me that he
could not and would not play with Richie because Richie was black. I was confounded —
I didn't know what to say."**

Exclusion is a part of everyone's life at some
point. Some believe it is human nature. Co-
medians tell the story of the man who is
found after having been stranded alone on a
deserted island for more than ten years. He takes his
rescuers on a tour of the island. The first structure he
takes them to is quite well built and he explains
that it is the house of worship. Next, he shows them
his home. Next to his home is a third structure.
Again, he refers to this hut as a house of worship.

Knowing that he has lived alone for ten-plus years, they look at him quizzically. He explains, "Oh, the first one is where I pray — it is the synagogue I belong to. The second is the one I don't belong to."

How can we help our children understand that it is okay to be selective, to have preferences, or to make friends based upon legitimate standards but not on characteristics over which a person has no control?

Examine what it feels like to be excluded. Imagine you are invited to spend an evening with people you've met before but don't know very well. You spend a good deal of time getting ready for the evening, wanting to make a good impression. You arrive on time and notice you're the only one dressed casually. Already you're feeling a bit on the outside. But you forge ahead. You say hello to people who return your warmth with blank stares. People all around you are engaged in conversation, but you can't seem to interest anyone in hearing what you have to say. You go home very confused, doubting yourself and trying to figure out what you did wrong. After several evenings like this, you finally get up the courage to approach one of these new acquaintances and you ask him why you can't seem to penetrate this group. He laughs nervously and finally admits that while everyone will indeed be polite to you, they'll never let you in because, you're not "one of them."

Most likely you'll turn down the next invitation you receive from this group, seeking instead to be with people who will accept you for who you are.

What if this was a work situation rather than a social one? What if you had to experience this feeling every day, nine to five? Could you handle it? What if the option of changing jobs did not exist? What would you do? This is what the excluded child faces. Day in and day out, the excluded child is forced to go to school where with any luck he or she is just ignored and left out. More likely, the exclusion will go further. It will include the teasing and joke telling we've already addressed, or even violence of some kind. How can you help your child get through this? Or what if your child is one of the perpetrators? How do you impress upon him or her just how awful this is?

Explore the Expressed Reason for Exclusion

When exclusion issues arise, parents need to begin their response by exploring the expressed reason for exclusion from both sides:

"Why did you leave Tony out?"

"Tony, why do you think you were left out?"

Listen carefully to what you are hearing as the answers are given. Some young people have no problem in loudly proclaiming their discrimination, while others will hide behind false reasons. As adults we need to ensure that we are neither overreacting to a particular circumstance nor underreacting.

Parents and primary caregivers are usually brought into exclusion issues either as the adult responsible for the perpetrator or for the victim.

Responding to the Perpetrator

"He can't come to our house, he's a _____."

"She talks funny, I'm not playing with her."

"It's my party, I'll invite whom I want, and I definitely don't want them."

We may be shocked to hear these and similar statements come out of the mouths of our children. It may be hard to believe such people are alive and well in your living room or at your kitchen table. Do not ridicule or silence them. Our role with both younger and older children who practice excluding others is to assist them in distinguishing between reasons that are legitimate and those that are not.

If the exclusion is based on a negative behavior (for example, not sharing, shoving), this legitimate issue should be brought up with the excluded child. Asking him or her not to behave inappropriately and pointing out to the child that others no longer want to play or hang out with him or her unless these behaviors are changed usually goes a long way toward cleaning up the causes for exclusion. Few people, young or old, want to be left out or prohibited from participating. To be deemed acceptable, they are only too willing to correct their behaviors unless the correction calls into question one of their primary values. It is not okay to let such behavior go on. Your comments to the victim who is justifiably excluded might go something like this:

"I understand that Michael and the other boys wouldn't play with you on the playground today. That must've felt pretty bad, huh? I talked with them and I think I know why. Yesterday, when they did play with you, they thought you were pretty bossy. They

said that you made them feel that everything had to be your way or no way. You might want to think about that. I am sure if you are ready to play fairly, they'll give you another chance. May I tell them we talked and that you are going to try harder not to be so bossy today?"

If you determine that the exclusion is based on characteristics over which the excluded child has no control (for example, race, religion, body size), help the excluders understand this and find positive reasons for including the child. One way to accomplish this is to start by asking the perpetrators what things are important about being a good playmate or friend. Younger children will usually list such items as:

◆   Being able to share

◆   Not hitting

◆   Liking to do things that I like to do

◆   Being able to do things that I am able to do

◆   Being funny

◆   Being nice

Older children will list more specific characteristics, such as:

◆ Trustworthiness

◆ Intelligence

◆ Considerateness

◆ Is fun

◆ Possesses similar interests

◆ Has similar values

Ask the perpetrators which of those items they can automatically cross off the list about the person they are excluding, based upon what they know about the person. If all they know is the person's skin color or religion or sexual orientation, they will discover that they cannot automatically eliminate that person.

If, on the other hand, they feel confident that they can exclude the person based on such items as skin color or size or economic class, it is time to discuss stereotyping.

Another possible way to reach the incorrect excluder is to challenge him or her with questions such as, "Can he change the color of his skin?"

"Can you change the color of yours?" "Do you think that skin color has anything to do with being a fun playmate or a good friend?" "Have you ever tried befriending someone who was different from you?" Your conversation might go something like:

"Let me make sure that I understand why you don't want to include that person [those people]. It's because of what? Why would you think that this person is not good just because he has a certain color skin or practices a certain religion? Would you feel good about being excluded because of the color of your skin? Your religion? Think about someone you like very much. What makes him or her fun? Are you sure that this person doesn't possess any of these same traits? You only see his or her skin color, not the person inside. How do you know if he or she is someone you'd want to be around or not? Sometimes it is difficult or even a bit scary to talk with people who are different from you. That is just because you haven't had a chance to get to know them. Get to know them, and then if you don't like who they are — not what they are — you can make the choice not to include

them. However, I think you'll be surprised to find that good people (and bad people) come in all sizes, shapes, colors, and religions."

Discuss How Exclusion Feels

Often, our children are so busy trying to fit in themselves that they may not consider the feelings of their victims. It is important that you attend to your child's ability to empathize — to be able to "walk in another person's shoes."

When Your Child Is the Victim

The other exclusion situation arises when your child is the victim:

"He said I wasn't invited because I am a _____."

"They don't let girls in, only boys."

"I'm good enough to play ball with, but they never invite me to go out with them or go to their homes."

You may be bursting to tell your child that if those kids don't want him or her around, they don't deserve to know your child. But this statement will not get you too far with your child. Even young children want to fit in, and for most teenagers fitting in is a primary objective. Many children experience the pain of exclusion at some point in their lives. When the basis for this exclusion is something over which they don't have any control, the pain intensifies. An excluded child asks, "Why do I have to be _____?" It is critical that you help your child through this painful experience, not just console him or her.

The first step in your response must be to reassure your child that he or she does indeed have worth. If you are talking with a younger child, you can actually brainstorm a list of things that he or she can do, as well as draw up a list of people who care about him or her. The abilities list will affirm talents, and the caring list will affirm that he or she is acceptable to some people. If the child is older, start by offering direct reassurance and then see if together you can list at least two or three things that he or she likes about himself or herself.

Next, help your child identify a list of successful others who share the primary characteristic that has placed your child in exclusion. Identifying role models can be extremely helpful.

In both cases, you need to work with your child to develop a plan of action for confronting the bias that has led to the exclusion. Your conversation might go something like:

"It is so hard when people you like hurt you by excluding you, isn't it? You're probably pretty angry and hurt right now. I know I feel that way, probably because I love you and I know they are missing out on including a really great guy. It isn't very fair, is it? I would imagine you're not feeling too great right now, huh?"

"Imagine we don't know each other at all and you're writing to me and telling me why I would like you. What would you say? Now let's talk about how we might help your friends see those characteristics alongside the ones over which you have no control. In what ways might we help them see past their stereotypes to see who you really are?

"Remember, lots of times people form stereotypes out of the fear they feel about what they do not know or do not understand.

Do you think it might help if we tried to work on eliminating those fears by educating them?"

We have to recognize that some people can't be — or don't want to be — educated. And we should never put education before our children's safety. That said, we believe most people are capable of learning to respect differences. No matter how subtle the changes we can make are, they're a start. Sometimes, even when we think our efforts have failed, we have planted the seeds of understanding.

Ensure that your child has basic "friendship skills." Does he know how to introduce himself? Does she know how to form a relationship with someone she thinks might make a good friend? Does he have ideas about the traits that might make good friends or the warning signs that might indicate a poor choice? If she does successfully form an initial connection, does she know how to maintain and grow it? Has he developed the fine art of showing he cares without being overwhelming or clingy? Does she know how to give her friends "space"? What if a friend turns out not to be someone he feels good about being close to; does he know how to end their friendship?

It is a good idea to pose these questions and discuss possible solutions with your child at a time when emotions are not high. It is particularly important to do so with a child who is being excluded. He or she may be seeking some rules or assistance for forming friendships. Be very careful not to leave your child believing that he or she is being discriminated against or excluded based on factors that are in some way the child's fault or failure.

Zooing

"Why do Indian women wear those funny dresses?"

"Do you ever wish you had normal hair — you know, hair that wasn't so kinky?"

"Why do your men wear those ugly hats, and what's with the curls of hair by their ears?"

Children realize that people are not alike, and they are naturally curious. But when they show inordinate curiosity or ask insensitive questions — in slang, referred to as "zooing" — feelings can be hurt. Questions about differences become insensitive when a negative value is attached to the difference.

Sometimes children unknowingly fall into zooing when they simply mean to ask for information. If they seem as if they're making a judgment, you might want to say,

"We often think others are strange simply because they are different from us. We don't think our own beliefs and appearances are strange because we are used to them. We must seem strange to someone who is different from us."

Children who fall victim to zooing — to being asked insulting questions — often ask their own questions, such as:

"Mommy, why do they always want to touch my hair?"

"How can I get them to stop staring at my _____?"

Just as we can teach our children basic diversity skills, we can prepare them for the fact that not all people have mastered those skills. Rather than waiting until our children experience this negative behavior, talk with them about it in advance:

"Remember when we talked about the importance of asking questions — of seeking answers to things you may not understand about people who are different from you? Well, sometimes when people are faced with something they do not understand and they don't know how to ask questions appropriately, they ask insulting questions or fail to ask at all — they just stare. If this happens to you, it is important to try to figure out if the person meant to insult you or not. Don't assume that he or she did. If you feel it is safe and you feel able to, you might respond to an insulting question by directly asking, 'Do you really want to know something about me, my traditions, customs, or heritage, or were you asking because you were trying to put me down?'"

Summary of Advice for Parents About Excluding, Zooing, and Other Inappropriate Behaviors

- **Explore and determine the expressed reason for exclusion from both sides.**

- **Assist your children in distinguishing between reasons that are legitimate and those that are not.**

- **Find positive reasons for including the child.**

- **Discuss how exclusion feels.**

- **If your child is the victim, reassure her that she does indeed have worth.**

- **Ensure that your child has basic "friendship skills."**

- **Recognize that some people can't be educated and some acts of exclusion can't be solved. Always put your child's safety first.**

- **Be very careful not to leave your child believing that it is in some way his fault that he is being discriminated against or excluded based on factors beyond his control.**

CHAPTER 13

Crimes of Hate: Physical and Emotional Violence

"I had thirty seconds until the bell would ring, and I ran to my locker to get a book. I reached for the combination lock and froze. A swastika was painted on my locker. My eyes were fixed on the image as overwhelming evil stared back at me. I felt the symbol radiate intense animosity. I faced the emblem of genocide, of Nazi Germany, the emblem that called out, 'JEWS DIE.' I stood there in front of my locker motionless . . . furious and deeply hurt. The bell rang."

"We had just moved into our house a few months before. We got home late that night. As we pulled into the driveway, my father thought he saw someone in our backyard carrying a light. He walked around to the front of our house. In our mailbox were eggs and shaving cream. There was garbage in the road and on the front lawn. Written on our driveway were the words 'Spic Go Home.' And in our living room window was a bullet hole."

"I couldn't believe that one of the older guys — I think he was in seventh grade — called me a gook. We got into a fight. I had to hit him — he called me that name. The principal didn't care why I hit him — fighting is against school rules. We were both suspended."

"About an hour and half into practice, five guys showed up at school, near the band room. They were harassing one of the drummers, who is black. They were yelling racial slurs and telling him to come out and fight. Soon more guys showed up yelling . . . eventually there were twenty of them. We were so scared."

"When you're biracial, it feels like you're getting it from everyone. Hard as it is to have your whole town hate you, it's even worse when your family, your own flesh and blood, is leading the pack. Most of my dad's family are KKK members. They threatened my mom's life, they threatened to harm us, they killed both my dogs. Keep in mind that I was only seven, my brother five, and my sister two."

"In August of 1993, my life changed forever. My best friend, Joel, was murdered. He was murdered because he was gay. He went for a walk and never came home. Instead, his life was ended by a man who thought he was doing the world a favor by ridding our society of gay men. He killed three other men and injured another before he was caught."

Perhaps your child is part of the lucky majority that has not been the direct victim of physical or emotional violence or has not lost a friend to it. Yet few children today have not been touched by it. In our work with literally thousands of students, we have yet to find a teenager who could not cite an example of hate-related violence that he or she had either experienced, witnessed, read about, or seen on television. Their feelings about these incidents have run the full gamut — from empathy with the victims to support for the perpetrators and from disgust for the haters to personal fear.

Our children are living in a world that includes hate-related violence. We can't afford to pretend it doesn't exist or wait until it hits our front door to address it.

Setting the Rules on Violence

D o you remember hearing one or both of your parents saying something like, "What you do someday in your own home will be your decision, but as long as you live under this roof you will live by the rules of this home?" A discussion about hate-crime and bias-related violence should begin with a review of the rules of your house. You may not think your children are always listening, but when we asked the students in our workshops to

How America Stands

**AMONG INDUSTRIALIZED COUNTRIES,
THE UNITED STATES RANKS:**

1st   in military technology

1st   in military exports

1st   in Gross Domestic Product

1st   in the number of millionaires and billionaires

1st   in health technology

1st   in defense expenditures

10th in eighth-grade science scores

14th in the proportion of children in poverty

16th in living standards among our poorest one-
      fifth of children

16th in efforts to lift our children out of poverty

17th in low birth-weight rates

18th in the gap between rich and poor children

21st in eighth-grade math scores

22nd in infant mortality

Last in protecting our children against gun
violence

tell us the rules for how people treat one another in their homes, here's what we heard:

"Be nice. No hitting. No spitting. No punching. No biting. Sharing is good." (from first graders)

"Remember the golden rule — treat others how you would like to be treated. No name-calling. No ethnic jokes. No interrupting. No fighting." (from middle-schoolers)

"Respect is mandatory. No harassing. No touching without permission. No violence." (from high-schoolers)

All of the young people could name the rules. But when we probed a bit, they were confused. A question such as the following was really hard for first graders to decide:

"If you are only playing around and tap someone lightly, is it against the rules?"

Even more difficult for our first graders and our middle-schoolers were questions like,

"What if you get hit first? Is it okay to hit back? How about if you are standing up for a friend?"

The high school students could not all agree on where the line is drawn between teasing and harassing, playing and hurting.

Start a conversation about violence by reviewing the rules and discussing what they mean. Your children can contribute to the conversation and can affirm or expand the list of rules. It will help you learn what is confusing to them, and it may also offer you a glimpse of what they are experiencing each day but not telling you about:

"So here I was, reminding Jason for the umpteenth time that it is not okay to hit, when he responded by telling me, 'I know, Mommy, Mrs. Jacara tells us that all the time in school. That's why she got so mad last week when Niah hit Rebecca in the face and broke her nose.'"

"'I know you don't think it is ever okay to hit,' said my seventeen-year-old son, Garfield, 'but if the guys don't stop calling me a nigger, I'm not sure I can follow that rule.' I didn't know the guys were calling him nigger."

Next, reach consensus on what you consider physical and mental violence. When does an action cross the line into violence? Ask your children to make a list of examples of actions they think are violent. Discuss them. See if you can determine their rationale for classifying the action as violent:

"Okay. You said that when Tommy punched Charlie in the nose he was being violent. How about when Jim pushed John on the basketball court the other day? Was that violence? How about when Cheryl made the little girls give her all of their desserts at lunch — was that violence? Or when the kids who sit in the back of the classroom were shooting spitballs at the kids who sit in the front of the room, was that violence? If you and Dad are wrestling on the floor, is that violence?"

What about threatening? Do you have rules about threatening? How do you respond when your four-year-old says,

If you don't make me breakfast, I'm going to punch you."

Or when you overhear your teenage son say to his younger sister:

"What's up with that? You mean you're gonna hang with those guys? They're spics. I'll beat your ass if you hang with those guys."

What do you say? Where is your line? Where are the lines for your children? Do they coincide?

Review your rules and see if they are specific enough. Do your children know your expectations of them beyond their own behavior? What do you expect them to do if they see someone else being victimized? Or if their peers are urging them to get violent? What about if they're not there when the violence occurs but hear about it afterward? How do your expectations change if the victim is a family member? Can you justify an older brother resorting to violence if he learns that his younger sister was the victim of verbal abuse by one of his friends? Your conversation should not end until you are both sure that you've been understood and are clear on the rules and expected behaviors.

If Your Child Is
Being Victimized

If you suspect your child is being victimized, you must find out. Often, our children are embarrassed to admit they are the targets of someone's hate. They somehow interpret telling you as showing a sign of weakness, another vulnerability at an already vulnerable point. As with drug and alcohol abuse, there are times in the lives of our children when it is better to pry — to ask more questions than you normally would — than it is to close your eyes to what may be very dangerous for your child.

In the past few years, we have seen extremist youth-perpetrated violence. While the incidents are statistically low, if your child was one of the victims, the numbers would not matter. According to a recent *New York Times*/CBS Poll (October 1999), 52% of American teenagers think their school could experience the kind of massacre that devastated Columbine High School in Littleton, Colorado. Statistically, youth violence is lower than it was at one time. However, the daily threats and acts of intimidation are not captured in the statistics. And threats can be equally scary and hurtful.

Ask Questions

If you think your child is being threatened or bullied, don't wait to be told — ask him or her. If you ask, the worst thing he or she can do is deny it. If you don't ask and it is happening, the worst thing could be a lot worse.

"You seemed a bit afraid when I got to the playground today. Did something happen?"

"What was Cathy saying to you when I walked over? You seemed scared."

"I heard that Michael has been threatening some of the other black kids. Has he done that to you?"

Offer Help

Believe your child if he says he's being bullied, and make sure he knows you believe him and want to help. When our children are afraid, they need to know we understand, we believe them, and we are there for them. Don't tell your child to "get in there and fight." A lot more than a black eye may be at stake. Do not assume your child can handle the situation alone. Talk through possible responses and contact the appropriate authorities or school officials for help. Do not take threats lightly or decide not to report them because you are embarrassed. Remember, your child has a right to live without threats or bullying. No one has the right to scare or intimidate him.

"It must be so scary to be bullied like that, and I bet it makes you angry, huh? I am glad we're talking about it because you matter so much to me and I want to see if together we can figure out what to do."

Unless your child has truly provoked someone into threatening him or her, be careful not to blame your child and be sure your child does not blame herself.

"Sometimes when bad things happen to us, we wonder what we did to bring them on. This is so foolish because we don't usually ask for bad things to happen. I am sure you did nothing to bring this on yourself."

Don't Keep It Secret

Don't promise to keep the bullying a secret. Secrecy may prevent you from doing anything about the problem. If you do promise secrecy, you must honor your word.

"I know you may be scared or even embarrassed by what is happening. I promise I won't tell everyone about it, but I will need to tell people who can help to resolve the problem, okay?"

If you know the child making the threats or doing the bullying, and you feel either the child or his or her parents are approachable, then do discuss the issue with them. However, if not, do not assume that confronting them is necessarily the best answer.

ACCORDING TO THE CENTERS FOR DISEASE CONTROL AND PREVENTION, U.S. CHILDREN UNDER AGE 15 ARE:

16 times more likely to be murdered with a gun

12 times more likely to die from gunfire

11 times more likely to commit suicide with a gun and

9 times more likely to die in a firearm accident than children in 25 other industrialized countries combined.

Common Questions

Three common questions asked by children who have experienced being threatened because of their race, religion, ethnicity, sexual orientation, physical abilities, and so on, are:

"How can we tell without everyone thinking I'm a snitch?"

"Sometimes it is more important to be safe than to be concerned with whether or not people think you are a snitch. I can understand that you don't want people to think you'd rat out someone — but in this situation, it is right to tell. Imagine if this situation were happening to your best friend and there was something you could do about it. Wouldn't you want to do what you could? Well, in order to help, you'd have to know it was happening, right? Telling the teacher or the principal is really just turning to someone who can help — someone who is in a position to do something."

"Why should I let them see that they hurt me?"

"There is nothing wrong with being hurt. They gave you very good reason to feel hurt. If you can't admit how you are feeling or are afraid to let others see it, then they have robbed you of that right. Don't let them rob you of that. You have not done anything wrong and have no reason to be embarrassed or ashamed. If you are worried that they'll get some sick satisfaction in knowing that you're hurt, remember that is their problem — not yours."

"Maybe I should just stick to my own kind. I bet this wouldn't happen then, huh?"

"Why do you want to let them take away your right to hang out with whomever you want? Besides, if you trust only your own kind, you are doing what they are doing — judging people only by traits over which they have no control."

When Your Child Is
the Perpetrator

Sometimes, much to our disappointment, it is our own child who is doing the harassing or threatening. Some will give the excuse that they were only kidding:

"Why can't people just toughen up — not be so sensitive?"

Others will claim that it was the peer pressure that made them do it:

"I was either in on it — or a victim of it. I couldn't stop the guys from what they were doing, I was too afraid myself."

Yet others will accept full responsibility, at times with pride:

"So what . . . she was one of 'them' — who cares what I did to her?"

We cannot ignore these behaviors, regardless of the reasons for them, when they hurt someone. Just because peers expect us to go along with them does not make us innocent. And even if our child truly believes "they" deserve it, no one deserves it. We must react strongly and let our child know that this behavior is not acceptable on any terms.

All forms of harassment and violence are difficult to negotiate. Bias-related violence or hate crimes are uniquely horrific because not only is the individual victim hurt by them, but all people who share the trait on which the perpetrator decided to act also feel vulnerable, hurt, and victimized. Your child may be a victim by association.

"When I saw the swastikas on my synagogue and the words 'DIE JEW' spray painted across the doors, it was as if someone had punched me in the stomach. For the first time in my whole life I didn't feel safe in my town. I wished we would move away."

"I heard that they were targeting gay men. They'd already beaten two guys that I knew. I know a lot of people don't approve of my life. They don't like what I am. But there's a big difference between not liking my life and

trying to end my life. I don't think I've ever been that scared before. I was afraid to come out of my house."

"At first I read about the fact that someone or a bunch of someones were burning down black churches. Then we talked about it in my social studies class and I began to wonder what it would be like if on Sunday I learned my church had been one of them. Our churches are God's houses — they're holy places. When they burn down our holy places, they burn us, too."

In the aftermath of a hate crime in our community, or one that takes place elsewhere but hits home, we must talk with our children. Don't assume that they are unaware of what is happening around them. Children across America feared going to high school the day after Columbine's horror. Many Jewish parents worried about their preschoolers the day after the daycare center in California made headlines because a hater struck there. People are victimized when attackers go after "people like them." In such situations, we must ensure that:

◆　our children receive the support necessary to feel safe;

◆　they are provided opportunities to express how they are feeling;

◆　whenever possible, they are given a means by which to channel their feelings into positive actions;

◆　if necessary, real safety precautions are put into place.

Ensuring these factors may require:

◆　arranging for group discussions either in school or in other locations where youths congregate, hopefully facilitated by a professional;

◆　calling upon leaders of the victims' community (for example, a rabbi if the victim is Jewish, the president of the local NAACP or Urban League if the victim is African-American, a representative from GLADD if the victim is gay, etc.) to talk with groups of our children to let them know others are concerned as well;

◆　brainstorming a list of actions that our children can undertake if they choose to. These might range from reaching out to the family members of the actual victims to creating workshops that youth peer leaders can facilitate to writing letters asking for hate crime legislation, etc.

Remember when your child's biggest fear in life was handled by turning on the night-light? Now it takes more than being there to turn on the light, to chase away the imaginary monsters from under the bed. Unfortunately, the fear is of real people in the school cafeteria or on the bus. But we can bring children the light of understanding and preparation. We can be sure they know what can happen and are ready with responses.

CHAPTER 14

Key Diversity Skills
and Concepts

Our world is changing so rapidly, it is virtually impossible for us to be well-informed or vigilant enough to teach our children all they need to know about all of the cultures that exist today. We can't prepare them for every possible form of bias they may encounter. We can, though, gather tools from the examples we've seen here to use in our efforts against hate. There are two basic diversity skills that can help both ourselves and our children cope with any "new" situation we might face and ten key concepts to remember.

Basic Diversity Skills

I t's all about questions and answers — *respectful* questions that lead to answers that promote *understanding*. Our work begins at home, in talking to our children with respect and understanding. If we do that, they will learn the two basic skills they need to meet the differences they will find in the world outside:

1.   The ability and willingness to ask questions — to be both comfortable and sensitive enough to formulate questions about what they do not know about people who are different from themselves.

2.   The ability and willingness to give answers — to be both comfortable and knowledgeable enough to provide the information about themselves, their cultures, and heritage that others may be seeking.

As basic as these skills are, mastery of them requires practice. You can help your children acquire and refine these skills by giving them the guidelines below and by practicing with them.

Asking Questions

Consider your question before posing it and think through how it will be heard. Ask yourself, would I answer that question if it were posed to me? What would it take to make me comfortable enough to provide an answer? Would someone close to me have to ask or would I answer to an acquaintance, coworker, or stranger? What tone of voice or body language might help me to know if the asker is sincere in his or her search for an answer? Would I answer publicly or would I be more apt to respond if it was a private conversation?

Any question that starts with the words, "How do all _____s feel about . . ." is in and of itself a biased question. It implies that all _____s feel the same way — that they are in some way a homogenous group or voting bloc, committed to expressing only one view or employing only one school of thought. And yet we hear these questions daily. Students of color (especially those who are in the minority within their educational institutions) hear teachers ask questions such as, "Kevin, how do black men feel about the candidates?" Or our newspaper headlines ask, "How do women feel about abortion?" as if all women share the same opinion.

Check out the appropriateness of a question by inverting it so that it asks for the same information from a different group. GLADD, a nationally known organization committed to fighting homophobia and heterosexism, put out a list of questions traditionally asked of gay, lesbian, and bisexual adults, posed instead for heterosexuals. As you read through their list of revised questions, you understand how biased they are in their original form. The list includes such questions as, "Is your heterosexuality a phase and how old do you think you will be when you outgrow it?" "Do you think your heterosexuality might be overcome through therapy?" "Do you think you are a heterosexual because you had a dominant mother or a dominant father?" Similarly, you can hear the bias of the "How do all _____s feel about . . ." when you fill the blank with a majority group.

Try to pose questions to original sources — not secondhand sources — whenever possible. Instead of asking a friend of the Chinese girl in your class about a particular Chinese custom, ask the Chinese girl herself. After all, she might be a great resource.

Answering Questions

Help your children find ways to impart information about themselves, their cultural and religious beliefs, and so forth, before the questions are even posed. Practice formulating brief but complete answers.

Assist them in finding ways to comfortably decline answering when they feel they can't or really don't want to. Often, our children find themselves fed up with being the "answer givers" — with having to serve as the cultural educators. This is particularly the case when your child is one of only a few people like herself (or the only one) amid a larger population of people who share a common race, culture, or religion. This frustration is very real. As educators in classrooms across the country can attest, some kids are asked the same questions umpteen times a day by their peers, adding up to an incredible number of times they are forced to give the same answers over and over.

It is still important, when possible, to give answers regardless of the frustration. This is best explained through an experience we had delivering anti-bias education to a corporate client:

"We arrived on day 1 of what would be months of training different groups, to learn that each day the company would provide a lunch consisting of a huge international buffet. Not wanting to get tired of the same meal over and over, the training team decided that we would 'eat from a different country' each day. Around day 18 or 19 we found ourselves standing in front of a table that had a huge bowl filled with spinach leaves and something orange and chunky. Not being familiar with the dish, we asked what it was.

" 'Oh,' said the server, 'that's our African-American dish.'

" 'What is it?' we asked.

" 'Well, that's sweet potato salad,' he replied.

"Not having ever had it before, we turned to the African-American members of our training team and inquired, " 'What is the significance of sweet potato salad to the African-American culture?'

"No one knew. We decided to do a bit of research. We checked libraries and informa-

tion lines. We called chefs and magazine editors. No one could answer our question. Finally, one of our trainers suggested that we call a real expert on the topic — his grandmother. So we called grandma.

" 'Grandma,' we asked, 'what is the significance of sweet potato salad to the African-American culture?'

" 'Child,' she replied as only a grandma can, 'there is no such thing as sweet potato salad in the African-American culture!' "

The moral of the story is that unless we provide accurate information about our cultures and beliefs, you can be assured that someone else will fill in the gaps with made-up information. Americans are notorious for this. Chop suey does not exist outside of the United States — it was invented in San Francisco. Pizza in Rome is not what gets delivered here as an Italian dish. We assign foods as well as other things to cultures arbitrarily until enough people believe it and thus it becomes a fact.

If we want the world to understand who and what we are, we must be able and willing to provide answers. Help your children distinguish between questions of genuine and idle — or insensitive — curiosity and prepare responses for times when they feel frustrated or overwhelmed.

Encourage your children to admit what they do not know. This is hard enough for adults. For children it may be especially difficult. Their schooling has brought them to a place where they feel they must know the answers. We must help them understand that accuracy is more important than giving the asker the impression that they possess an expertise that they do not have.

Ten Key Concepts About Hate

1. Recognize that hate hurts everyone. Starting with yourself, work to raise awareness about the genesis and contagion of hate.

2. Even though hate is persuasive and commonplace, understand that there are positive steps you and your children can take to combat it; we are not powerless in the face of hate.

3. Work hard to help your children feel good about themselves. People who feel good about themselves exhibit less prejudice and discriminatory behavior than people who don't.

4. Look to role models for inspiration. Understand that "whistle-blowers" are risk takers, and assess your best strategies for taking action against hate, especially in situations where hateful speech and behavior is the norm.

5. Find ways to maintain momentum in the fight against hate. Look for allies in the community for support, and work to support others.

6. Hold yourself to the same high standard you have for your children. Be honest and consistent in your behavior.

7. Recognize that unlearning biased messages is a process. Allow for mistakes in yourself and others.

8. Recognize that we need to educate boys and girls in ways that allow for their full humanity. By the time children enter kindergarten, the boys have been taught in various ways that they need to adopt a stoic, macho stance, a "boy code" that views showing sadness as weakness and acting out as masculine.

9. Teach your children the two basic diversity skills: The ability and willingness to ask questions, and the ability and willingness to give answers.

10. Learn to see all of this nation's children as *our* children. We must provide hopeful futures for all children so that we can create a future of respect and understanding for all.

Part Three

Challenging Hate Outside the Home

Introduction

No one needs to tell us that today's world is vastly different from the world in which most of us grew up. While many of us lived in homes with a television set, there were a limited number of stations and they all went off the air at some point. With the advent of cable and satellite dishes, television is now available twenty-four hours a day, with literally hundreds of station and programming choices, many of which do not adhere to the family-appropriate standards of traditional television. Whereas before we could limit our children's access to programs we deemed appropriate, today our desktop computers and Internet lines open our homes to people and organizations of all kinds that might entice our children to support their beliefs and ideologies. Moreover, without a filtering system, our children are left to navigate this information highway without necessarily being prepared to distinguish fact from fiction.

The changes are not limited to technology. With more parents choosing to or being forced to work, most children are left to their own devices for longer periods of time. Our houses of worship no longer serve as the sole centers of our communities. Our schools are no longer charged with teaching only the three R's but now with trying to fill in the gaps by meeting the needs of their students through life skills instruction, counseling, and mediation. Teachers are trying to fit such things as conflict resolution and anti-bias skill development into an already too-tight day, while not neglecting their other academic responsibilities. Moreover, the diversity of the student populations they are trying to serve may require the infusion of a number of teaching techniques and lesson plans to ensure that all children are provided an equal education.

Almost all parents want the same basic things for their children. We want them to be healthy. We want them to be safe. We want them to be happy. We want them to achieve success. While we may define health, safety, happiness, and success differently, hate in a child's life (experienced either as a perpetrator, as a victim, or even as a witness) can impair the possibility of achieving any of these goals. Just as we have seen with other bias-related issues, it is imperative that we talk to our children about hate outside the home, in our schools, in the media, and — in its most recent incarnation — on the Internet.

CHAPTER 15

Combating Hate
in Schools

"While school is usually a safe place, sometimes something happens that makes you feel unsafe. In the early nineties, the area around my school was exploding. I went to Clara Barton High School, on the edges of Crown Heights, Brooklyn — the place where the tensions between the black and the Jewish communities were so bad that people took to rioting in the streets. I wasn't sure what would happen at school. Fortunately, my COSA (Coordinator of Student Activities), Ms. Cuttle, was interested in how we — the students — were feeling. She got an offer of help from the Anti-Defamation League and right away followed up on it.

"Together, the ADL and Ms. Cuttle created and implemented a Peer Training Program. Twenty-eight of us were taken through a process whereby we confronted our own biases and then learned anti-bias skills. Once we were ready, we then learned how to teach what we had learned to our peers and to younger children.

"The program has grown over the years. Today, there are over 1,000 peer trainers in New York City alone, working to eradicate prejudice. We deliver workshops in school, at churches, synagogues, and mosques, at youth group meetings, anywhere kids get together, and sometimes we even give them for parents. It shows you what can happen when a teacher cares and a school works with a nonprofit to support her concerns. Schools, nonprofits, parents, and the community working together have really made a difference."

Parents, children, and educators all want schools to be safe places where every student can learn in an atmosphere of inclusion and respect. Too often tensions based on differences enter classrooms, playgrounds, and cafeterias, creating divisions that inhibit learning and sometimes even lead to violence. Parents and children can both be active participants in promoting respect and fighting hatred and bigotry in our schools.

What Parents Can Do

◆ Talk with your children and ask them how safe they feel their school environment is. Do they feel safe? Do they see hatred being ignored or responded to? Is the general climate one of respect for differences?

◆ Find out about the school's policy on bias-related incidents and disciplinary action. Discuss the policy with your children and help them understand the reasons behind the rules as well as the consequences for breaking them.

Responding to Hate

PLAN AHEAD

- **Work with school and community officials and law enforcement personnel to establish a plan for responding promptly to hate crimes and incidents.**

- **Educate community and school staff on how to recognize hate-motivated incidents.**

- **Establish clear procedures for reporting hate-motivated incidents and crimes and disseminate the information communitywide.**

- **Train school and community counselors to assist victims of hate-motivated incidents.**

- **Provide referrals to community organizations that offer counsel and support services in these situations.**

RESPONSE STRATEGIES

- **Notify law enforcement.**

- **Be sure of the facts.**

- **Conduct a complete investigation of the incident, including the questioning of the victim(s), witness(es), and perpetrator(s). Report hate-motivated crimes to law enforcement.**

- **If there is physical damage (for example, defacing, spray painting), take photographs.**

- **As soon as the damage has been viewed by law enforcement and photographs taken, offer assistance in repairing or cleaning up the damaged or vandalized property.**

- **If hate literature has been distributed, collect the literature for evidence.**

- **Notify the Anti-Defamation League and similar agencies in the appropriate communities.**

- **Reach out to the victims with expressions of concern and support and reassure them and their families that the incident will be treated seriously.**

- **Gather signatures on a petition repudiating the act.**

- **Organize coalitions to march, protest, or sponsor a public forum to discuss the specific incidents and plan active measures to prevent a recurrence.**

- **If the incident occurred in a school, work with the school administration to determine appropriate disciplinary actions.**

◆ Be involved in your children's school life by supporting and reviewing homework, talking with teachers, and attending school functions such as parent conferences, class programs, open houses, and PTA meetings. If you have concerns about biased curriculum or treatment, report them to the appropriate members of the faculty or administration.

◆ Work with your children's school to make it more responsive to all students and to all families. Plan ways parents can help represent and encourage diversity in the classroom and in before- and after-school programs.

◆ Request that anti-bias skills and diversity education programs are available to your child. These
life skills are crucial to their ultimate success and
may not be provided if not requested.

Parent Participation

**"My daughter's teacher asked me to do a Chanukah
presentation next week for her third grade class. I'm
delighted! What a change this is from when I was in
elementary school, where only Christian holidays were
acknowledged. . . . What are some guidelines I should
follow while sharing holidays in the classroom?"**

**Be pleased that Lisa's teacher is trying to rec-
ognize Lisa and make her feel special in a positive
way, while providing all her students with an understanding that differences are to be valued, not
rejected.**

**The basic guideline you need to remember is
that the public schools can teach *about* religion as
long as they do not promote a particular religion.
You should feel comfortable telling the story of
Chanukah, explaining its significance to the Jewish
people and giving the class some experience with
the holiday — by reading an age-appropriate story,
for example, or serving latkes, or giving the history
of the dreidel and playing the game."**

◆   Find out if your employer sponsors parent participation in school activities.

"While teachers and administration may be key to establishing the educational atmosphere in our children's schools, parents can't afford to wait for them to take the lead if that atmosphere is not conducive to the best learning for all children. At the same time, if we speak out only as individuals, we are too easily dismissed. We have to organize — across race, class, and other societal barriers — and learn to speak with one voice on the issues of importance to us. Only then will we see the changes that are necessary to make our schools places of growth and achievement for all children."

— **Susan Naimark, from**
The Role of White Parents in
Overcoming Racism

What Children
Can Do

◆ Recite a pledge against prejudice at a school-wide assembly.

A WORLD OF DIFFERENCE®
Institute Pledge

I pledge from this day onward to do my best to interrupt prejudice and to stop those who, because of hate, would hurt, harass, or violate the civil rights of anyone. I will try at all times to be aware of my own biases against people who are different from myself. I will ask questions about cultures, religions, and races that I don't understand. I will speak out against anyone who mocks, seeks to intimidate, or actually hurts someone of a different race, religion, ethnic group, or sexual orientation. I will reach out to support those who are targets of harassment. I will think about specific ways my school, other students, and my community can promote respect for people and create a prejudice-free zone. I firmly believe that one person can make a difference and that no person can be an "innocent bystander" when it comes to opposing hate.

◆   Display a poster-size version of the pledge in a prominent area of your school and encourage people to sign it.

◆   Establish a Diversity Club that serves as an umbrella organization to promote harmony and respect for differences. Reach out to sports teams, drama clubs, and language clubs for ideas and involvement.

◆   Initiate classroom discussions of terms such as anti-Semitism, racism, sexism, homophobia, and bias.

◆   Invite a motivational speaker who is a recognized civil or human rights leader to address an all-school assembly. Videotape the speech and publish an interview with the speaker in the school and local newspapers.

◆   Organize an essay contest whose theme is either a personal experience with prejudice or a success story in the fight against it. Suggest that the winning entries be published in your school newspaper and featured in your town newspaper or highlighted on a local cable TV program.

◆ Create an antiprejudice slogan for your school that could be printed as a bumper sticker and sold in the wider community to raise funds for these efforts.

◆ Hold a Rock Against Racism or other concert, a dance-a-thon, bike-a-thon, car wash, or battle of the bands, and donate the proceeds from ticket sales to underwrite diversity training and other programs for the school.

◆ Form a student–faculty committee to write Rules of Respect for your school and display the finished set of rules in every classroom.

◆ Invite your district attorney, police chief, or a representative from the state attorney general's office to speak to your school about civil rights, hate crimes, and other legal aspects of the fight against prejudice.

◆ Designate a wall space on or near school grounds where graffiti with a harmonious and unifying message can be written, drawn, or painted.

◆ Publish a newsletter specifically devoted to promoting respect for diversity and publicizing multicultural events. Try to have your local newspaper or community Internet home page do the same.

◆ Encourage representation of all students on every school board, committee, club, publication, and team.

◆ Write an original song/chant/rap that celebrates your school's diversity, and perform it at school rallies and other events.

◆ Create a flag or poster that symbolizes your school's ideal of diversity, and display it at games, assemblies, and other school events.

◆ Hold a T-shirt contest to come up with a logo or slogan like "I Don't Put Up With Put-Downs." The winning T-shirt design could be printed and sold at your school bookstore or in local shops, at community events, or sports competitions.

◆ Create a calendar with all the holidays and important civil rights dates represented in your school community.

◆ Participate in a poster campaign such as ADL's You Can't Turn Your Face Away from Hate that encourages people to intervene when confronted with instances of prejudice.

◆　Create an orientation program that addresses the needs of students of all backgrounds so that they feel welcome when joining the student body.

◆　Initiate a pin drive in which students look for pins with positive slogans and tack them onto a designated bulletin board in the student lounge or other central gathering place.

◆　Poll your teachers about their ethnic and cultural backgrounds and their experiences with prejudice. Ask each to write a short paragraph on the subject that can be compiled in a faculty book.

◆　Produce a Proud Out Loud video comprised of interviews with students and their grandparents about their ethnic heritage and why they are proud of it.

◆　Host a poetry slam in which students read aloud original poems or raps that break down stereotypes and promote respect for diversity. Invite participants to present their work to PTA meetings, Chamber of Commerce events, and other community groups.

◆   Research prodiversity Web sites. Then build a Web page for your school and link it to others on the Internet.

◆   Contact ADL about monitoring hate activities on the Internet.

◆   Create a student-run Speakers Bureau, where students of different backgrounds speak about their heritage.

◆   Devise a skit contest with themes that promote diversity.

◆   Turn a school assembly into a game show for students of all grades called Cultural Pursuit. Ask teachers to develop questions covering every discipline and hold "culture bees" in their classrooms to determine assembly contestants.

◆   Devote time in art classes to designing a Diversity Quilt with each patch representing a student's individual heritage. Have all classes combine their patchwork squares to form a school quilt for display in the community.

◆   Organize a No-Ethnic-Humor Open-Mike Nite featuring stand-up comedy by students.

◆　Meet with food services at your school to discuss the possibility of featuring ethnic cuisines on a regular basis. Consult with local restaurants and community groups to participate in the program.

◆　Construct a multimedia display that examines how today's media perpetuate stereotypes. Consider current films, television sitcoms, music, and advertising campaigns in addition to newspapers, magazines, and books.

◆　Research peace negotiations going on around the world regarding ethnic or racial conflict. Then stage a Mock Summit in which students take on the roles of international leaders and try to resolve these crises.

◆　Look for examples of youth who have struggled to overcome oppression throughout history and create an original dramatic performance based on their experiences.

◆　Sponsor a Dance for Diversity and approach a local radio station about broadcasting live from your event.

◆   Establish a school exchange that matches students from different schools to bring youth of differing backgrounds closer together.

◆   Start an annual multicultural film festival at your school. Invite community groups and local theaters to be cosponsors.

◆   Re-create the Ellis Island Immigration Station for a schoolwide event. Involve teachers from all disciplines to create period costumes and scenery and to prepare traditional foods. Issue passports to all students attending and lead "new immigrants" through the interview process.

◆   Collect samples of popular teen magazines and comic books from around the world. Ask your librarian to set aside a special corner for them in the periodical room.

◆   Research children's books representing the experiences of different ethnic groups. Then initiate a reading program with a local bookstore or library that features these books.

◆   Survey local card and gift shops for product lines geared to diverse groups. Write to greeting card companies and local merchants to advocate for expanding the diversity of selections. Coordinate a contest to create a line of cards and/or note paper that promotes respect for diversity.

◆   Approach the guidance office about hosting a career workshop led by professionals who can discuss diversity in their respective fields.

◆   Ask your school to host an Internship Fair for groups such as ADL and other civic organizations that hire student interns.

◆   Advocate for the production of school plays that are sensitive to multiculturalism and incorporate a variety of roles and perspectives representing a diverse cast, audience, and story.

◆   Ensure that the musical selections of school bands and choruses are culturally diverse.

◆   Speak to each of your teachers about posting a list somewhere in the classroom of famous pioneers and leaders in their field with a special focus on diversity.

◆   Collect famous speeches about civil rights. Put them together in a binder or in a video collection, and then make it available to your whole school community.

◆ Research civil unrest in this country, from rebellions during the time of slavery to Chicago in the 1960s to Los Angeles in the 1990s.

◆ Survey the colleges in your area about their diversity and affinity clubs. Invite a panel of representatives to speak to the senior class of your high school about "Prejudice on the College Campus: What to Look for — What to Do."

What Teachers and Administrators Can Do

- **Examine your own cultural biases and assumptions. Explore your perceptions and understanding of situations by developing an awareness of your cultural "filters."**

- **Integrate culturally diverse information and perspectives when working with young people. Relegating equity issues to a special or "multicultural" time sends a message to children that such issues are unimportant relative to other activities in which you and the children are involved. Explore diversity issues and incorporate multiple perspectives on a regular basis.**

- **Allow time for the process to develop. Introduce less complex topics first and create time to establish trust. Develop ground rules for discussion that allow for honest dialogue within a respectful context. Recognize that the long history of mistrust between people in different groups will not dissipate quickly.**

- **Establish an environment that allows for mistakes. Since most of us have unconsciously acquired prejudicial and stereotypical thinking, we may not be aware that certain attitudes are harmful to ourselves and to others. Acknowledge that intolerant thinking will surface from time to time in ourselves and in others. Model nondefensive responses when told that something you said or did was offensive to someone. Assume goodwill and make that assumption a common practice within your groups.**

- **Intervene. Be prepared to respond to purposefully directed acts of bias. Children will carefully observe how you intervene when someone is the target of discriminatory and hate-based behavior. Your silence in the face of injustice conveys the message that you condone the behavior or consider it not worthy of attention. Your appropriate and timely intervention is critical in establishing an environment where all children feel valued and respected.**

- **Keep learning.** Keep abreast of current issues and discuss them with children. Clip articles from newspapers and magazines and post them in the classroom. Let children know that you consider yourself a learner in these issues.

- **Avoid preaching to children about how they should behave.** Research indicates that exhortation is the least effective method for changing prejudiced attitudes; in fact, it often produces a result opposite from the desired effect. Encourage children to resolve conflicts, solve problems, work in diverse teams, and learn new information about themselves and others through interactive experiences.

- **Encourage empathy.** Encourage children to share life experiences and choose literature that will help them develop empathy. Make your school or center a place where children's experiences are not marginalized, trivialized, or invalidated. It is not fruitful to engage in a debate over who has suffered the most. Oppression is harmful to all people in all of its forms.

- **Review resources.** Review material so that displays and bulletin boards are inclusive of all people. Ensure that books and videos you use do not reinforce existing stereotypes. When you encounter such examples, point them out to children and encourage a discussion about them.

- **Make a home-school-community connection. Involve** parents, caregivers, family members, and other members of the community in the learning process. Understand that families and other community members provide the context in which children learn and are motivated to learn. Examine how you can connect home, school, and community with one another and the larger world.

"I now make a commitment that I will not tolerate racism, bigotry, and anti-Semitism, that I will stand up and protest for what is right. I will share my thoughts and ideas with the people in my community, my school, my city, and my nation." — Manuel Fuentes, New Orleans Delegation, ADL's 1999 National Youth Leadership Mission

CHAPTER 16

Combating Hate in the Media — TV, Movies, Books

"It is impossible to keep kids away from the media messages of our culture! Sometimes we give ourselves a false sense of security by telling ourselves that we can!"

— Mother of a five-year-old daughter, Washington, DC

Sometimes we parents would like to forget that our children have learned things that we have not taught them. Children absorb the spoken and unspoken messages of our society on an ongoing basis. We can't protect them from the onslaught of these messages, but we can help them understand and interpret what they are seeing, hearing, and reading.

Screening Television and Movie Messages

◆ **Know what your children are watching.** Think about what values and images you want permeating your home. Assess the values of television programs and movie videos by watching them first without your child and asking yourself if they support your family's philosophy. (You can tape good TV programs for viewing together later.)

◆ **Become media literate.** Help your children make sense of what they see. Young children, especially, often cannot distinguish between a dramatic production on the screen and the news. They are easily deceived and manipulated by advertisers. Use television and movie stereotypes as "teachable moments." Point out stereotypical and manipulative images when you see them and tell your children why such images are harmful. It is just as important to teach your children *how* to watch TV and movies as it is to monitor *what* they watch.

◆ **Become consumer savvy.** Understand the relationship between commercial advertising on TV and public responsibility. Let television executives know what you think about the programming on their networks. Teach your children how to complain about inequity and offensive programming in the media.

◆ **Don't give your TV the power to keep your family from talking.** Six out of ten families in the United States eat dinner with the TV on. Choose to be in the minority by turning off the TV during dinner and using the time to talk and listen to one another.

TV and Movie Questionaire

Use the following questionnaire to help assess group representation and stereotyping in television programs and movies. Talk with your children about the patterns they see. Do the heroes or heroines always belong to a certain racial or ethnic group? Are the males always brave and the females always afraid? Does one group always "win"? Use your findings to discuss fairness and bias in media messages.

Name of Movie/TV Program _____

Questions	African-American Male/Female	White M/F	*Other (specify) M/F
1. How many major characters are there?			
2. Who are the heroes/ heroines?			
3. Who are the villains?			
4. Who is smart and capable?			
5. Who creates problems?			
6. Who solves problems?			
7. Who is brave?			
8. Who is afraid?			
9. Who seeks help from someone else?			
10. Who fights?			
11. Who is successful?			
12. Who is passive or reserved?			
13. Who leads?			
14. Who follows?			

*Create other categories to examine other forms of stereotyping.

Time Children Spend Watching TV

- **Children in the United States watch an average of 3 to 5 hours of television each day.**

- **Prime-time television shows depict an average of 5 to 6 violent acts per hour, and Saturday morning children's programs show an average of 20 to 25 violent acts.**

- **Only 10% of children's viewing time is spent watching children's television. The other 90% is spent watching programs designed for adults.**

Evaluating and Selecting Children's Literature

A nalyzing children's books for hidden stereotypes is particularly important because children are interested in a story's plot and characters and are unlikely to consider whether a book includes biased messages. If young children are repeatedly exposed to such messages, there is a danger that they will come to accept them as "true." Parents can help children select literature that is both entertaining and accurate.

Multicultural children's literature should serve as both a mirror to children and a window to the world around them, teaching them to appreciate their own heritage as well as the heritage of others. No single book can represent all forms of diversity, but there can be an appropriate balance in a collection of books. Here are some guidelines to use:

Story Line

1. Are the stories interesting to children?

2. Are the stories realistic (unless they are fantasies or fairy tales)?

3. Are there various conflicts for children to explore?

4. How are the conflicts presented?

5. How are the conflicts resolved?

◆ Are conflicts resolved only through the intervention of a person from a dominant group?

◆ Are people from other groups considered to be "the problem" or the cause of the conflict?

◆ Are various responses to conflict depicted?

◆ Do boys as well as girls resolve conflicts?

◆ Do children as well as adults resolve conflicts?

Characterization

1. Are characters realistic and depicted as genuine individuals?

2. Do characters represent individuals from a variety of cultural groups?

3. Are characters of color represented as authority figures and in decision-making roles?

4. Are females as well as males depicted in leadership roles?

5. Are characters multidimensional or do the stories focus only on such traits as race, ability, gender, sexual orientation, or religion?

Theme

1. Do story lines offer children a variety of things to think about, question, and consider?

2. Are values being explored instead of preached?

3. Are there lessons to be learned?

4. Do the themes presented reflect a variety of cultural values?

Setting

1. Do the stories reflect a variety of settings?

2. Are urban, suburban, and rural settings represented realistically?

3. Are cultural settings represented realistically?

4. Are there clear distinctions between children's lives in the United States and children's lives in other countries?

Language

1. Are texts appropriate for the reading ability and age of the children?

2. Is the language appropriate for the time and place of a particular story?

3. If texts are bilingual, does English always appear as the primary language at the top of the page, followed by a second language?

4. Does the language reflect the authentic language of children or the language of adults speaking for children?

Historical Accuracy

1. Are historical events depicted accurately?

2. Are various perspectives on historical events reflected?

3. Are there noticeable omissions of historical information?

4. Does the information given reflect the most recent scholarship?

Illustrations

1. Are diverse populations and settings represented?

2. Is there diversity represented within cultural groups?

3. Are characters realistically and genuinely represented?

4. Are illustrations engaging?

Other Considerations

1. Do the positive characteristics of a particular book outweigh the negatives?

2. Will the stories encourage discussion?

3. Are children exposed to multiple perspectives and values?

4. Do the stories promote a better understanding of a diverse society?

In the Resources section at the end of this book (page 319) is a selected bibliography of multicultural children's books listed by age group.

"I am seventeen years old. I am a Native American. And everything my friends know about my culture they learned from TV. They keep asking me where my feathers are — when do I paint my face — is my father a chief — do I live in a tepee? I wish just once television would show a Native American who happens to be a lawyer or a doctor or a teacher or something. We are regular people, you know."

CHAPTER 17

Combating Hate
on the Internet

" . . . any person with a phone line can become a town crier with a voice that resonates farther than it could from any soapbox. Through the use of Web pages, mail exploders, and newsgroups, the same individual can become a pamphleteer. As the District Court found, 'the content of the Internet is as diverse as human thought.'"

— Supreme Court Justice John Paul Stevens

"When I signed online on Chanukah to wish my friends a happy holiday, this was the first greeting I received: 'Kike, Jew Girl, Brown-nosing Jew.' I was devastated and crushed. How could anybody be so hateful, so ugly, and so blatant toward me? What had I done wrong? I ran with my legs shaking and tears running down my face to my mother and father."

— Sixteen-year-old girl

Many parents are troubled by the increase of hateful material on the Internet. Children who explore the Internet, whether visiting Web sites, reading e-mail messages, or "conversing" in chat rooms, run the risk of encountering hate propaganda. Many hate groups specifically target young people, and their hateful messages can have a big influence on our children.

"If your child gets an assignment to write a paper on the Holocaust and decides to use the Net as his or her research source, you may be amazed at what you get. Along with great historical and factual information, your child will also be directed to Holocaust denial sites — sites that preach anti-Semitism and other forms of hate. Some education, huh?"

Hate is very accessible on the Internet. Using simple search tools, young Internet users can easily find hate propaganda. They may also stumble on it inadvertently. Misleading extremist Web sites that may lure unsuspecting children are on the rise.

A kid searching for activity pages might land at a white supremacist site devoted to children, complete with coloring pages and a crossword puzzle.

Hate propaganda, from subtle to heavy-handed, is aimed at influencing attitudes and behavior. At the extreme, anti-Semites and racists use the Internet to recruit new, young members. Online membership forms are found at several hate sites, making it easy to join. Likewise, it is simple to order hateful books, CDs, jewelry, and other items using the Internet. Some hate sites even offer links to bomb-making pages, which could potentially contribute to violent actions.

What Parents Can Do

Parents need to help their children deal with on-line hate through discussion and education. Parents should become active participants in their children's Internet experiences. Some ways to achieve this include:

◆ Asking questions that encourage discussion about what your children are seeing on the Internet.

◆ Encouraging your children to ask questions about material they do not understand.

◆ Exploring Internet sites with your children.

◆ Paying attention to the sites your children are exploring. Something as simple as having the computer in an open area or facing an open door can give you information without prying.

◆ Making yourself knowledgeable about hate on the Internet by direct research online and through publications such as ADL's *Poisoning the Web.*

◆ Many major Internet companies and nonprofit organizations are offering services to protect kids from encountering hate online. Ask whether your Internet provider has safeguards or advice, or contact organizations such as the Anti-Defamation League.

◆ Choosing to install ADL HateFilter™ on your home computer. The HateFilter protects children by blocking access to World Wide Web sites that advocate hatred, bigotry, or violence on the basis of race, religion, ethnicity, sexual orientation, or other "differences."

Regulation of speech on the Internet by the international community or any one government would be virtually impossible, both technologically and legally. In the United States, the First Amendment of the Constitution guarantees the right of freedom of speech to all Americans, including the vast majority of extremist Web sites that disseminate racist or anti-Semitic propaganda. However, the First Amendment does not protect speech that threatens or harasses specific people or speech that libels individuals or organizations by name. Internet users need to let ADL and other responsible authorities know about threatening, hateful, and violent messages and materials that they find.

What Children Can Do

ere are six tips you can give your children to help protect them online:

1. If you see any threatening or bad language on-line, be sure to report it to a parent, librarian, or teacher.

2. Do not give out your home address, telephone number, or school name without asking a parent, and never share personal information online (for example, in a chat room or newsgroup/message board post).

3. Never accept e-mail, files, or URLs from strangers.

4. Keep your passwords a secret. Don't even tell your best friend.

5. If you feel unsafe or uncomfortable, notify your parents, librarian, or teacher, and leave the chat room or Web site.

6. Do not agree to meet someone in person without asking a parent first.

Conclusion

As a powerful technological tool that permits instant communication between many different populations around the globe, the Internet can help educate people and promote messages of understanding and respect that bring us all closer together. By staying involved in and informed about your children's Internet explorations, you can help ensure that these explorations are positive learning experiences, not lessons in hatred and bigotry.

CHAPTER 18

Making a Commitment to Change

> "I have a dream that my four little children
> will one day live in a nation where they will
> not be judged by the color of their skin but
> by the content of their character."
>
> — **Martin Luther King**, Jr.

Beyond teaching our children how to resist bias in their everyday lives, we need to show them the power of positive, concerted action. Addressing the roots of prejudice in our communities, workplaces, and houses of worship sets an example of courage and hope for the future of our society, the future that our children will inherit.

There is no cookie-cutter solution to the challenge of educating against the ignorance that leads to prejudice, bigotry, and discrimination. We need to try a variety of approaches. Comprehensive approaches — approaches that attack bias through numerous networks simultaneously — stand the greatest chance of having institutional impact.

When an entire community commits to and implements a comprehensive approach, real change begins. We recommend that you reach out to and mobilize a broad-based coalition to ensure the success of your efforts against hate in your neighborhoods, houses of worship, and workplaces. Enlist the support of peers, family members, school administration and faculty, elected and appointed officials, religious and business leaders. Encourage your children to join in activities that will give them the sense that they can indeed make a difference.

In Your Community

◆   Establish a Human Rights Commission and a Community Watch Group in your city or town.

◆   Organize a local multicultural committee that serves as an umbrella committee for groups that raise awareness about prejudice and provide support for cultural events, holiday programs, or community efforts that promote intergroup harmony.

◆ Volunteer to serve on one of these organizations and work to support their initiatives.

◆ Petition government officials to issue a proclamation making your city or town a prejudice-free zone.

◆ Plan a communitywide Walk/Run Against Hate, in which sponsored participants would donate all monies pledged to an anti-bias or other human rights organization.

◆ Become aware of your local demographics and compare them to others around the state to better understand the diversity in your community.

◆ Hold a communitywide Human Rights Day. Contact representatives of the Reebok Human Rights Board, Amnesty International, and other human rights organizations to participate.

◆ Build a community float that promotes understanding and respect for the diversity of your community, and march in local and state parades. Contact parade officials to make sure that groups of all different backgrounds are invited to march.

◆ Suggest to your local newspaper that it devote a corner of the editorial page each month to at least one opinion piece relating to antiprejudice and pro-diversity themes.

◆   Meet with school and community librarians and local bookstores to discuss ways to highlight literature that is representative of all cultures.

◆   Compile a citizen's directory of the businesses and community organizations that exist to support diverse groups in the community.

◆   Research your community's involvement in struggles for civil and human rights throughout our history, such as abolition, the civil rights movement, and so on, and create an exhibit for the local library or town hall.

◆   Discuss alternative accessibility routes such as ramps, stairs, and elevators in your community, and invite speakers into your school and community to talk about such initiatives.

◆   Make sure your public facilities accommodate the needs of all residents.

◆   Collect traditional family recipes from local residents for a community cookbook. Solicit ads to support the cost of reproducing and distributing the book as part of a welcome wagon for new residents.

◆ Organize a communitywide Hoops for Harmony basketball tournament with proceeds from ticket sales going to a local nonprofit organization that promotes awareness of and respect for diversity.

◆ Hold a Paint-Out Day to eliminate graffiti that promotes bigotry, culminating in a potluck supper.

In Your Workplace

◆ Make respect for diversity a core value in your company, and articulate it as such in the employee handbook.

◆ Provide ongoing awareness programs about the value of human diversity for all employees in the organization.

◆ Take advantage of diversity consultants and training programs such as A WORLD OF DIFFERENCE® Institute's A Workplace of Difference™ to assist with ongoing education.

◆ Incorporate diversity as a business goal. Secure a high degree of commitment from all employees.

◆ Become aware and respectful of individual work styles.

◆ Create an environment conducive to the exploration of diversity.

◆ Learn about your coworkers' backgrounds and share your own.

◆ Create a display area where employees can post notices of events and activities happening in their communities.

◆ Publish and distribute to all staff a list of ethnic and/or religious holidays and the meaning of the customs associated with celebrating them.

◆ Sponsor a "brown bag" luncheon lecture series that features speakers on diversity issues.

◆ Sponsor a mentoring program, and reach out to students in local high schools and colleges.

◆ Provide opportunities to attend local cultural events and exhibits.

◆ Participate as a sponsor in community events that support the health and welfare of society.

In Your House of Worship

◆   Urge your leaders to use the pulpit to condemn all forms of bigotry.

◆   Encourage friends of other faiths to visit your religious services, and share your religious knowledge with them.

◆   Invite clergy representing different religions to participate in your services and deliver the sermon.

◆   Host a tour for elected and appointed officials to learn more about your religion and the programs and activities your religious community offers.

◆   Ensure that all faiths are represented accurately in existing library materials and religious school curricula.

◆   Reach out to diverse religious communities to cosponsor festivals and holiday observance, such as ADL's Interfaith Seders, that highlight and celebrate our common humanity.

◆ Be respectful of everyone who attends your religious services whether they are members of or visitors to your congregation.

◆ Turn one bulletin board into a display space where newspaper and/or magazine clippings depicting current events related to anti-Semitism and other forms of religious persecution or human rights violations can be posted for all to read.

◆ Organize an interfaith retreat for young people to increase understanding of one another's beliefs and build lasting friendships.

◆ Plan an interfaith youth group trip to the U.S. Holocaust Memorial Museum in Washington, DC. Raise funds to cover travel expenses with a community bake sale, car wash, service auction, or other activity.

Comprehensive approaches against hate start with one person commited to putting such a plan in place, and they continue as he or she recruits others and garners the necessary level of commitment. It takes time. It takes work. But aren't our children — and their future — worth it?

Resources

Organizations and Web Sites

ADL (Anti-Defamation
League)
823 UN Plaza
NYC, NY 10017
(212) 490-2525
www.ADL.org

ADL's A WORLD
OF DIFFERENCE® Institute
823 UN Plaza
NYC, NY 10017
(212) 885-7800
www.ADL.org

Center for the Prevention of
School Violence
20 Enterprise Street
Suite 2
Raleigh, NC 27607-7375
(800) 299-6054
(919) 515-9397
Fax (919) 515-9561
www.ncsu.edu/cpsv

Children's Defense Fund
25 E Street, NW
Washington, DC 20001
(202) 628-8787
www.childrensdefense.org

Educators for Social
Responsibility
23 Garden Street
Cambridge, MA 02138
(800) 370-2515
(617) 492-1764
Fax (617) 864-5164
www.npin.org/reswork/
workorgs/socialre.html

Family.com
www.family.go.com

Family Education Company
20 Park Plaza
Suite 1215
Boston, MA 02116
(617) 542-6500

Fax (617) 542-6564
www.familyeducation.com

Gay, Lesbian and Straight
Education Network (GLSEN)
121 West 27th Street
Suite 804
New York, NY 10001
(212) 727-0135
Fax (212) 727-0254
www.glsen.org

Leadership Education for
Asian Pacifics, Inc.
www.leap.org
327 East Second Street
Suite 226
Los Angeles, CA 90012
(213) 485-1422

Look Smart Categories
www.looksmart.com
Web site containing information about Bullying. Look
under the Personal category
and click on family

National Association for the
Education of Young Children
(NAEYC)
1509 16th Street, NW

Washington, DC 20036
(202) 232-8777
www.naeyc.org

National Conference for
Community and Justice
www.nccj.org
475 Park Avenue South
19th Floor
New York, NY 10016
(212) 545-1300

National Congress of
American Indians
www.ncai.org
1301 Connecticut Ave., NW
Suite 200
Washington, DC 20036
(202) 466-7767

National Council of La Raza
www.nclr.org
1111 19th Street, NW
Suite 1000
Washington, DC 20036
(202) 785-1670

National Italian American
Foundation
www.niaf.org
1860 19th Street, NW

Washington, DC 20009
(202) 387-0600

National PTA
330 North Wabash Avenue
Suite 2100
Chicago, IL 60611
(800) 307-4782
(312) 670-6782
Fax (312) 670-6783
www.pta.org

National School Safety
Center (NSSC)
141 Duesenberg Drive Suite 11
Westlake Village, CA 91362
(805) 373-9977
(805) 373-9277
www.nssc1.org

National Urban League
www.nul.org
120 Wall Street
8th Floor
New York, NY 10005
(212) 558-5300

Parents Helping Parents
3041 Olcott Street
Santa Clara, CA 95054-3222
(408) 727-5775
Fax (408) 727-0182

www.php.com
(children with special needs)

Stand for Children
1834 Connecticut Ave., NW
Washington, DC 20009
(800) 663-4032
(202) 234-0095
Fax (202) 234-0217
www.stand.org

Teaching Tolerance
Southern Poverty Law Center
400 Washington Avenue
Montgomery, AL 36104
(334) 264-0286
www.splcenter.org/teaching-
tolerance.html

United States Department
of Justice
950 Pennsylvania Ave., NW
Washington, DC 205301
www.usdoj.gov/kidspage

www.scholastic.com/
parentandchild
Web site that reprints articles
from the magazine *Parent
and Child*, published by
Scholastic Inc.

Selected Bibliography

Adults

Always Kiss Me Goodnight: Instructions on Raising the Perfect Parent by 147 Kids Who Know, Salt, J.S. Crown Publishing Group, 1997.

Anti-Semitism in America, Dinnerstein, Leonard. Oxford University Press, 1995.

Bullies & Victims: Helping Your Child Through the Schoolyard Battle, Fried, S. & Fried, P. M. Evans and Company, 1996.

Children Learn What They Live, Nolte, Dorothy. Workman, 1998.

Confronting Anti-Semitism, Zakim, Leonard P. KTAV, 2000.

Crossing the Color Line, Reddy, Maureen. Rutgers University Press, 1996.

Everyday Acts Against Racism, Reddy, Maureen. Seal Press, 1996.

40 Ways to Raise a Nonracist Child, Mathias, Barbara. Harper Perennial, 1996.

How to Talk So Kids Will Listen and Listen So Kids Will Talk, Faber, A. & Mazlish, E. Avon Books, 1991.

Is It a Choice? Answers to 300 of the Most Frequently Asked Questions About Gays and Lesbians, Marcus, Eric. Harper, San Francisco, 1993.

Jews Against Prejudice, Svonkin, Stuart. Columbia University Press, 1999.

Letter to a Jewish Friend, Svidercoschi, Gian Franco. Crossroad, 1994.

Lives of Notable Gay Men and Lesbians: Martina Navratilova. Zwerman, Gilda. Chelsea House, 1994.

Night, Wiesel, Eli. Bantam, 1982.

Peaceful Parenting in a Violent World, Cress, J.N. & Berlowe, B. Perspective Publications, 1995.

Positive Self-Talk for Children, Blotch, D. & Merritt, J. Bantam Books, 1993.

Prejudice, Muse, Daphne. Hyperion, 1998.

Racism Explained to My Daughter, Jelloun, Tahar Ben. New Press, 1999.

Raising Compassionate Courageous Children in a Violent World, Cohn, Janice. Longstreet Press, 1996.

Raising Readers: Helping Your Child to Literacy, Bailostok, S. Penguin Publishers Limited, 1992.

Richard Wright & The Library Card, Miller, William. Lee and Low, 1999.

Teaching/Learning Anti-Racism: A Developmental Approach, Derman-Sparks, Louise, et al. Teachers College Press, 1997.

Teaching Peace: How to Raise Children to Live in Harmony – Without Fear, Without Prejudice, Without Violence, Arnow, Jan. The Berkley Publishing Group, 1995.

Teaching Tolerance: Raising Open Minded Empathetic Children, Bullard, Sara. Doubleday, 1996.

The Sweeter the Juice, Haizlip, Shirley. Simon & Schuster, 1994.

There Once Was a World, Eliach, Yaffa. Little Brown, 1999.

Walking With the Wind, Lewis, John. Harvest/Harcourt, 1999.

What to Do When Kids Are Mean to Your Child, McCoy, E. The
    Reader's Digest Association, 1997.
Why Are All the Black Kids Sitting Together in the Cafeteria?
    Tatum, Beverly. Perseus, 1997.

For Preschool Age Level

Abuela, Dorros, Arthur. Dutton, 1991.
Abuela's Weave, Castaneda, Omar. Lee and Low, 1993.
All Kinds of Families, Simon, Norma. Albert Whitman &
    Company, 1976.
All the Colors We Are, Kissinger, Katie. Redleaf Press, 1994.
Arnie and the New Kid, Carlson, N. Viking, 1990.
Frozen Noses, Carr, J. Holiday House, 1999.
Hop Jump, Stolwalsh, E. Harcourt Brace & Company, 1993.
The Treasure Hunt, Cosby, Bill. Scholastic, 1997.
Whoever You Are, Fox, M. Scholastic, 1997.
Yoko, Wells, R. Hyperion Books, 1998.

For Elementary and Middle School Age Levels

A Chair for My Mother, Williams, Vera B. Greenwillow, 1982.
Amazing Grace, Hoffman, Mary. Dial, 1991.

Ashok by Any Other Name, Yamate, Sandra. Polychrome Publishing, 1992.

Aunt Harriet's Underground Railroad in the Sky, Ringgold, Faith. Crown, 1992.

Bajo La Luna Limon, Fine, Edith. Lee and Low, 1999.

Baseball Saved Us, Mochizuki, Ken. Lee and Low, 1993.

Behind the Secret Window, Toll, Nelly. Penguin, 1993.

Bein' With You This Way, Nikola-Lisa, W. Lee and Low, 1994.

Black Is Brown Is Tan, Adoff, Arnold. Harper, 1973.

Blue Jay in the Desert, Shigekawa, Marlene. Polychrome Publishing, 1993.

Calling of the Doves, Herrera, Juan Felipe. Children's Books Press, 1995.

Celebrating Chinese New Year, Goldsmith, Diane Hoyt. Holiday House, 1998.

Celebrating Kwanzaa, Goldsmith, Diane Hoyt. Holiday House, 1993.

Chicken Sunday, Polacco, Patricia. Philomel Books, 1992.

Children of Asian America, Yamate, Sandra. Polychrome Publishing, 1995.

Clambake, Peters, Russell. Lerner Publications, 1992.

Daddy's Roommate, Willhoite, Michael. Alyson Publishers, 1990.

Daniel's Story, Matas, Carol. Scholastic, 1993.

Erik Is Homeless, Greenberg, Keith Elliot. Lerner Publications, 1992.

Everybody Bakes Bread, Dooley, Noah. Carolrhoda Books, 1996.

Families: A Celebration of Diversity, Commitment, Jenness, Aylette. Houghton Mifflin, 1993.

Felita, Mohr, Nicholosa. Dial, 1979.

Friends in the Park, Bunnett, Rochelle. Checkerboard Press, 1993.

Going Home, Mohr, Nicholosa. Dial, 1986.

Going With the Flow, Blatchford, Claire. H. Carolrhoda Books, 1998.

Grandmother's Dreamcatcher, McCain, Becky Ray. Albert Whitman & Company, 1998.

Harry & Willy & Carrothead, Caseley, Judith. Greenwillow, 1991.

Heather Has Two Mommies, Newman, Leslea. Alyson, 1991.

Hiding From the Nazis, Adler, David A. Holiday House, 1997.

I See the Rhythm, Igus, Toyomi. Children's Books Press, 1998.

Journey Home, Uchida, Yoshiko. Macmillan Children's Group, 1982.

Just Like Me: Stories & Self-Portraits of 14 Artists, Rohmer, Harriet. Children's Books Press, 1997.

Kwanzaa Karamu Cooking and Crafts for a Kwanzaa Festival, Brady, April A. Carolrhoda Books, 1995.

Losing Uncle Tim, Jordan, Mary Kate. Albert Whitman & Company, 1993.

Mardi Gras: A Cajun Country Celebration, Goldsmith, Diane Hoyt. Holiday house, 1995.

Mufaro's Beautiful Daughters, Steptoe, John. Lothrop, Lee & Shepard, 1987.

Now We Can Have A Wedding, Cox, Judy. Holiday House, 1998.

Passage to Freedom: The Sugihara Story, Mochizuki, Ken. Lee and Low, 1997.

Peace Tales: World Folktales to Talk About, McDonald, Margaret Read. Shoe String Books, 1992.

People, Spier, Peter. Doubleday, 1980.

Rag Coat, Mills, Lauren. Little Brown, 1991.

Ramadan, Ghazi, Suhaib Hamid. Holiday House, 1996.

Rising Voices: Writings of Young Native Americans, Hirschfelder, A. B. & Singer, B. R. Scribners, 1992.

Sadako, Coerr, Eleanor. Putnam, 1993.

Sara's Secret, Wanous, Suzan. Carolrhoda Books, 1995.

Silent Observer, Mackinnon, Christy. Kendall Green Publications, 1993.

Somewhere Today: A Book of Peace, Thomas, Shelley Moore. Albert Whitman & Company, 1998.

Sweet Clara and the Freedom Quilt, Hopkinson, Deborah. Alfred A. Knopf, 1993.

The Brother's Promise, Harber, Frances. Albert Whitman & Company, 1998.

The Christmas Menorahs, Cohn, Janice. Albert Whitman & Company, 1995.

The Devil's Arithmetic, Yolen, J. Viking, 1988.

The Friendship, Taylor, Mildred D. Dial, 1987.

The Keeping Quilt, Polacco, Patricia. Simon & Schuster, 1988.

The Meanest Thing to Say, Cosby, Bill. Scholastic, 1997.

The Unbreakable Code, Hunter, Sara Hoagland. Northland Publishing, 1996.

This Is Our Seder, Hildebrandt, Ziporah. Holiday House, 1999.

To Be a Drum, Coleman, Evelyn. Albert Whitman & Company, 1998.

What's Your Name? Sanders, Eve. Holiday House, 1995.

White Lilacs, Meyer, Carolyn. Harcourt, Brace, and Company, 1993.

White Socks Only, Coleman, Evelyn. Albert Whitman & Company, 1996.

Who Belongs Here? An American Story, Knight, Margy Burns. Tilbury House, 1993.

Who's in a Family? Skutch, Robert. Tricycle Press, 1995.

For Middle and High School Age Levels

A Level Playing Field: Sports and Race, Hu, Evaleen. Lerner Publications, 1995.

Anne Frank Remembered, Gies, Miep. Simon & Schuster, 1988.

Anne Frank: The Diary of a Young Girl, Frank, A. Doubleday Dell, 1952.

A Sporting Chance: Sports and Gender, Steiner, A. Lerner Publications, 1995.

Battlefields and Burial Grounds, Echo-Hawk, R. C. & Echo-Hawk, W. R. Lerner Publications, 1994.

Chernowitz, Arrick, Fran. Penguin, 1983.

Civil Rights: The Long Struggle, Lucas, Eileen. Enslow Publishers, 1996.

Everything You Need to Know About Bias Incidents, Osburn, Kevin. The Rosen Publishing Group, 1994.

Everything You Need to Know About Discrimination, Palmer, E. The Rosen Publishing Group, 1995.

Growing Up Gay, Reed, Rita. WW Norton, 1997.

Heeding the Call: Jewish Voices in America's Civil Rights Struggle, Finklestein, N. The Jewish Publication Society, 1997.

Japanese-American Internment in American History, Fremon, D. K. Enslow Publishers, 1996.

Journey of the Sparrows, Buss, F. L. Lodestar Books, 1991.

My Grandma's in a Nursing Home, Delton, Judy & Tucker, Dorothy. Albert Whitman & Company, 1986.

My Two Uncles, Vigna, Judith. Albert Whitman & Company, 1995.

New Kids in Town: Oral Histories of Immigrant Teens, Bode, J. Scholastic, 1989.

Reach for the Moon, Abeel, S. Pfeifer-Hamilton, 1994.

Rights of Women, Wharton, M. Gloucester Press, 1989.

Straight Talk about Prejudice, Kranz, R. Facts on File, 1991.

The Relocation of the North American Indian, Dunn, J. M. Lucent Books, 1995.

The Singing Man, Medearis, Angela Shelf. Holiday House, 1994.

The Sneetches, Dr. Seuss. Random House, 1961.

Up to the Plate, Galt, M. F. Lerner Publications, 1995.

Voices from the Fields, Atkin, S. Beth. Little Brown, 1993.

Working Together Against Racism, Milios, R. The Rosen Publishing Group, 1995.

Zlata's Diary: A Child's Life in Sarajevo, Filipovic, Z. Penguin, 1993.

Grateful acknowledgment is made by the authors for permission to use/reprint the following:

Pages 1-5: Quotes from children from the video "Names Can Really Hurt Us." Licensed under the authority of WCBS-TV New York. ©1989 WCBS-TV; **Page 6:** Current U.S. Population Statistics, U.S. Department of Commerce, Bureau of the Census, Statistical Abstract of the United States, 1992; **Pages 9–10:** The article "Not in Our Town," February 16, 1996. Reprinted with permission from the *Long Island Jewish World*; **Page 13:** "You've Got to Be Carefully Taught," song from the Broadway musical *South Pacific* by Richard Rogers and Oscar Hammerstein II. ©1949 by Richard Rogers and Oscar Hammerstein II. Copyright Renewed. Williamson Music owner of publication and allied rights throughout the world. International Copyright secured. All Rights Reserved; **Pages 16–17:** Quote from *Developmentally Appropriate Practice in Early Childhood Programs,* p. 56. Reprinted with permission from the National Association for the Education of Young Children; **Pages 24–25:** Quote from *Developmentally Appropriate Practice in Early Childhood Programs,* p. 120. Reprinted with permission from the National Association for the Education of Young Children; **Chapter 1:** "Prejudice: A Big Word for Little Kids" (ADL/Minneapolis TV video) quoted throughout; **Page 68:** Some Religions of the World from "Teacher, they called me a ...!" p. 40. Reprinted with permission from the Anti-Defamation League; **Pages 79–80:** Sidebar from "A WORLD OF DIFFERENCE® Institute Youth Service Activity Guide," "Exploring Our Diversity," p. 45. Reprinted with permission from the Anti-Defamation League; **Page 83:** Quote from the National Association for the Education of Young Children's Anti-Bias Curriculum, p. 41. Reprinted with permission from Louise Derman-Sparks; **Page 84:** Sidebar from "Teacher, they called me a...!", p. 18. Reprinted with permission from the Anti-Defamation League; **Pages 139–140:** Sidebar from "A WORLD OF DIFFERENCE® Institute Youth Service Activity Guide," page xxvii. Reprinted with permission from the Anti-Defamation League; **Pages 155–157:** Sidebar from "A WORLD OF DIFFERENCE® Institute Youth Service Activity Guide," page xxxii. Reprinted

8177